Lightning Strikes

A Memoir

by

Steve Krulevitz

ISBN-13:978-1539370482

The Life and Times of

a Professional Tour

Tennis Player

For my wife Ann and

our daughter Stephannie

Special Thanks-

Patrick and Eliza Smithwick

John "Captain John Smith" Stoller

Miles "Davis" Calabresi

James "Popeye" Giza

Eileen "Ida" Lion

Rasmus Keinicke

Jeffrey Christ

PREFACE

Lightning

Lightning, a gigantic electrostatic discharge, is the nickname of my former tennis coach. In nature, lightning illuminates its surroundings and follows with booming thunder. My friend is similar. He lights up the faces of people around him, and follows with his booming voice; it's hard not to admire his power.

Steve Krulevitz grew up in Baltimore and attended Park School, as did I. He would wake at 5:00 a.m. to practice tennis so he could go to basketball, soccer, or lacrosse practice in the afternoon. In the spring he played both lacrosse and tennis. While at Park, he won the Maryland State Athletic Association tennis singles title four years in a row and led in assists his senior year in lacrosse. Professionally, he ranked number 42 in international singles tennis in the world.

After Krulevitz's professional career ended, he returned to Baltimore with a vision he developed on the professional tour. That vision was the Steve Krulevitz Tennis Program, a tennis program for kids of all ages and skill. This was the birth of Lightning.

At camp his energy was palpable. Instruction and improvement were important, but the child's wellbeing and happiness were his priorities. Lightning created nicknames for all at camp. It became their identity around Lightning. The monikers helped form bonds that lasted long after a session's end and way beyond the boundaries of the courts. Even today, many of my friends still call me Shredder.

Before I met Lightning I didn't like tennis much, but Friday afternoons quickly became the highlight of my week. With friends Jake the Snake, Speedy, and Coleslaw, the two-hour sessions ended too quickly. My tennis skills improved impressively, but I hardly noticed. I was too busy having fun competing in games that were Lightning specialties. I came back year after year and Lightning was always glad to see me; it made me feel special. Lightning made everyone feel this way.

Lightning's infectious attitude has permeated my life. I too believe that fun should be incorporated into nearly everything I do, and a positive attitude trumps most of life's challenges. I now use my Lightning-attitude and skill to make kids happy while teaching them squash. I learned early on how easy it was to lose the kids' attention on the court. They would start sword fighting with racquets or just sit down, disinterested or bored. This was an issue for most of the volunteer coaches. I decided it was time to channel my inner Lightning. I changed my lesson plans, invented point systems for drills, and awarded prizes. I stopped talking only when I was cheering or high-fiving. The kids started smiling and laughing, and I knew that using the techniques I had learned from Lightning were as successful for my squash players as they had been for me.

– Andrew "Shredder" Katz

Chapter 1

Lightning Strikes

"We're almost finished. Just a few more minutes. Here, try again. Stee-ee-ven," I am told.

"Bee-bee-bin," I say.

I'm five years old, and I can't pronounce my own name. I'm having my half-hour private speech lesson at my family's house in Baltimore. Every Wednesday afternoon, from 4:30 p.m. to 5:00 p.m. My speech therapist, Miss Rita, is patient with me. I can tell she's trying really hard. I am, too.

"Stee-ee-ven" Miss Rita says again, and I can see her white teeth clenched tightly together. I try to purse my lips and place my teeth together like hers.

"Bee-bee-bin," I say. I know the kids in the neighborhood are starting to gather in the alley. All I want to do now is run. Run down to the alley and play.

"Steven, try again," Miss Rita says, with a big smile. "Just one more time."

"Bee-bin," I say.

Just then my mom comes into the den. "I'll see you next Wednesday," Miss Rita says to me.

"Mom, can I go down and play with the kids in the alley?" I ask. Word had gotten out that Big Mike was in the alley down behind his house, at his basketball court. And he wanted to play. "Sure, honey. I'll call you in a little while for dinner."

Helen Lustick Krulevitz is my mom. Born in Washington, D.C. to Charles Lustick and Esther Clugman. Helen was the youngest of four girls. Freda, Sylvia, and Mimi were my mom's older sisters. In her youth, she spent a lot of time at the family's furrier store in Washington, D.C., on 11th and H Street. Esther "Nanny" Clugman was the brains and Charles "Pop" Lustick was the brawn.

It's June 1956. My family lives in a house on Park Heights Avenue just a few blocks from Pimlico Race Course, a thoroughbred horse racetrack in Baltimore, Maryland. It is most famous for hosting the Preakness Stakes, the middle leg of the horse racing Triple Crown, every third week in May.

I race down the alley to Big Mike's basketball court and suddenly, Ronnie Book is there, along with Stuart Snyder, Michael Wiener, Bobby Deckelbaum, Steve Hammel, Ronnie and Joel Sher, Barry Rowan, Neil Kahanowitz, Arnold Bornstein, and Carl Lichtenburg. The kids of the neighborhood start coming from all directions.

Today, Michael "Big Mike" Freedman is a successful lawyer in Baltimore. In 1956, at just ten years old, he was the neighborhood leader.

"Hi," Big Mike says to me. "Do you want to play ball with us?" I nod but don't say anything.

"What's your name?" Big Mike asks me. I look up at him. Right into his eyes. There's no way in a million years I'm going to say, "Bee-bin." So I just look at him. Then the Bookman, who is six years old, says, "Hey, what's your name?" But I'm not talking. No way. Big Mike and the Bookman look at each other. Their eyes meet, and it's clear they're both thinking, *what's wrong with this kid?*

The afternoon game is called "Running Bases." You know that game, right? It is when two catchers stand on two bases, about ten yards apart, and toss the ball back and forth to each other. The players have to run back and forth between the bases without getting tagged by the ball. The last player not tagged out wins.

Big Mike, of course, and Stuart Snyder — who is eight years old — are going to man the lines. Just as the game is getting ready to start, Big Mike says to me, "Hey, come stand behind me, and if the ball gets past me, get it before it goes into the street. But don't run out of the alley." *Easy enough,* I think, and give Big Mike a nod.

The game begins calmly. But soon enough it starts to get a little crazy. Kids are running all over, from one line to the other, trying to get on base. At one point, Stuart is running to try to tag someone, but Big Mike, who has lots of kids on his end, thinks he can pick one off, so he yells out, "Stuart, over here!" Stuart turns and fires the ball to him. But Stuart's a little off balance. Plus, we're using a pinky ball. Anyone who has ever played with a pinky ball knows that ball can have a mind of its own. The pinky ball leaves Stuart's hand and flies way over Big Mike's head, past me, and down towards the street.

Off I go, like a shot out of a cannon. I tear after that pinky ball and run it down before it gets to the street. Then I trot back over with the ball and flip it to Big Mike. All the other kids are staring at me. There's total silence. "Wow," he finally says, "you're fast."

Big Mike tosses the ball to Stuart, and just as it hits Stuart's hand, there's a loud clap of thunder, followed by a huge streak of lightning way out in the distance. Before the rest of the kids can even get back on the lines, down comes the rain. It is a typical late-afternoon summer thunderstorm in Baltimore. All of the kids scatter like mice, scurrying in every direction for shelter. All the kids, that is, except for me. I'm still standing in the same spot I was when I flipped the ball to Big Mike. Frozen. Not sure where to go.

The rain is coming down in buckets now. Then a huge streak of lightning flashes across the sky. Much closer this time. Followed by an enormous clap of thunder.

All of a sudden, I hear a voice yelling, "Lightning! Lightning! Lightning!" I look over in the direction of the voice, and, standing in his backyard, waving his arms frantically, is Big Mike. The Bookman is behind him, up on the back porch of Big Mike's house, safely out of the rain.

"Lightning!" Big Mike yells out to me again now that he's got my attention, motioning for me to come over. "Over here! Over here!" he says.

I run over to him. "Come on, quickly," he says. "Follow me." So I follow him up on to his porch for cover.

"Get under here, Lightning," he says to me.

Chapter 2

Who Needs Tennis?

My dad got me started in tennis just before my eighth birthday. He had played number two singles at the University of Maryland in the mid-1930s. After he graduated, he became one of the first Jewish students admitted to the University of Maryland School of Medicine.

Kenneth Kaciel "Casey" Krulevitz was my dad. He was a great, great father but he was something else. What a piece of work. The guy had a ton of ambition and drive. But he had his issues, for sure. We all do. If someone asked me to rate him as a father, I would give him an A, even with all his *mishigas* — which is Yiddish for "the craziness of this world."

Casey — my father, who I sometimes called "Dad" but usually "Casey" — let me know early on that tennis is a funny sport. The footwork is totally different from, let's say, basketball and baseball, or any other sport. Plus, you are out there all by yourself with no teammates and it's lonely. When you're a kid, tennis is not as much fun as team sports. The only way you are going to get into tennis and stay into it is if your mom or dad pushes you in that direction.

I would say just about all pro tennis players had parents who played a major role—Jimmy Connors' mother and grandmother, Andre Agassi's father, Serena and Venus Williams' father, Dick Stockton's father, Harold Solomon's father, and Mary Pierce's father. You get the picture. Casey is right at the top of that list. You don't graduate as one of the first Jewish students from the University of Maryland School of Medicine in 1941 without ambition, determination, and perseverance. The genes probably don't fall far from the tree.

Would I have gotten into tennis without Casey? Probably not. Would I be the person I am today without his support, love and vision for me? Probably not. Do I forgive Casey for standing directly behind me, at the fence, jiggling the change in his pocket while I was about to serve for every one of my tennis matches all four years of high school? Probably not. Are there enough pages in this book to say thank you for encouraging and pushing me to be a better person and athlete? Definitely not. Thank you, Dad.

As I got older and started coming up through the junior ranks, I listened to a lot of what Casey had to say about tennis. He had some good tips.

The dining room table is where he held court. "Tennis is like boxing," Casey would say. "Obviously, you're not getting hit in the head. But it is similar. One-on-one. Mano-a-mano. You have to train for tennis like a boxer. Run. Skip rope. Lift Weights. Practice is your sparring."

When I was eight, my dad picked Maurice "Maury" Schwartzman to be my tennis coach. Maury was a former teammate of my father's at the University of Maryland. He had played number one singles and gone undefeated all four years. When you had a lesson with Maury, the lesson was on, no matter how you felt or the weather conditions.

It's January 1958. There's snow as far as the eye can see. We are at Druid Hill Park in West Baltimore. There is only one partially cleared and dry tennis court in a row of twelve. The wind coming off the Druid Hill Park Reservoir is nasty. Indoor tennis clubs do not exist at this time. Nothing but the cold, a few frozen tennis balls, Maury and me. We are the only people crazy enough to be out there playing tennis.

Maury would bring me up to the net during my half-hour Saturday morning tennis lesson and say, "Steve, you have to start the racquet up by your ear. Then, you take it down to the basement as if you were on an elevator." Maury would show me how it was done by swinging at the thin air. "And from here, you go straight down Park Heights Avenue," he'd say as he followed through. "That's the way you hit the forehand." That was fifty-six years ago, but it seems like yesterday. A good teacher and instructor, like Maury, stays with you all your life.

Casey always told me that when it comes to individual sports, you can never be in good enough shape. That's because it's just you out there. No teammates. You are solely responsible for every single move you make.

I learned that lesson the hard way in my very first tennis tournament, the Mid-Atlantic Championships. I lost, 6-0, 6-0, to a kid named Richard Healey. He moon-balled me to death at the Congressional Country Club on River Road in Bethesda, Maryland, a suburb of Washington, D.C. It was June 1960. I had just turned nine years old.

That match was going to be "it" for me — the end of my tennis career. Finished. Done. *No más*. I mean, 6-0, 6-0, that's embarrassing. Baseball was my sport anyway. I just played tennis because it was fun. It helped with baseball, too, which was a bonus. Now I can concentrate on baseball, I thought. The Fallstaff little league baseball team I was on was undefeated. I was the star pitcher and sometimes played second base. Ronnie "The Bookman" Book, my best friend at the time, was our catcher. We had it going. I pitched, he caught. Who needs tennis? Good riddance.

"It's okay, Steve," my coach, Maury, said during our next tennis lesson. "It was a good experience."

Maury was a great teacher. By the time of his death in 1994, he had taught tennis in the Baltimore area for nearly sixty years and was perhaps the most admired, respected, and beloved tennis instructor the city will ever know. Other local students of his included Elise Burgin and Andrea Leand, who both went on to have successful careers on the women's pro tour in the '80s and early '90s.

During his group clinics, Maury would buy a Coke for any kid who hit twenty-five balls in a row. That bribe wound up costing him a fair amount of dough. Of course, in those days you could get a Coke for a nickel.

After my loss at Congressional, Maury wasn't panicking. He was positive. I was not.

"This is my last lesson," I told him.

"What do you mean?" Maury said.

I looked down at the court. Couldn't look him in the eye. "I think I'm quitting tennis," I said, almost in a whisper.

"It's okay Steveo," Maury said. "It's just one tournament and your first ever." I just kept looking at the court. Who needs tennis?

"I'll make a deal with you," Maury said. He was really into it now. "Next week, there's another tournament. This one is here in town at Clifton Park. It's not very far away. You play that tournament, and if you still feel the same, then it's okay with me to quit, deal?" He stuck out his hand.

I looked up at him and smiled. "Sure, Mr. Schwartzman," I said, shaking his hand. "I'll play one more."

The following week was the first round of the boys' 10-and-under Baltimore Municipal Tennis Championships. I played the number one seed, who was a chunky little boy — and I mean *little* — from Silver Spring, Maryland. His name was Harold Solomon.

Even though Harold was only eight years old, he was ranked number one in the boys' 12-and-under division of the United States National Lawn Tennis Association (USNLTA) Mid Atlantic Section, which included Maryland, Washington, D.C., Virginia, and part of West Virginia. The USNLTA is now called the United States Tennis Association (also known as the USTA).

I lost the first set, 6-2. I had lost to Richard Healy, 6-0, 6-0. Now I was losing to Harold Solomon, 6-2. Enough is enough. Buckle down. Start fighting. Be steady. I started coaching myself just like Maury would in our lessons. I won the second set, 6-3.

Now it's 4-3 in the third set. I go to change sides and see that Harold is crying like a baby. He is bawling his eyes out. "Are you all right?" I ask him. He doesn't look over at me. "Are you okay?" I ask again. He still won't look at me. He's staring over at the parking lot, crying, and repeating over and over again, "My father is not here. My father is not here…"

His father, Leonard Solomon, had never missed a match—until today. Never in his wildest dreams would Leonard have thought that Harold would have any trouble in his first-round match. He had dropped Harold off at the red clay courts of Clifton Park in Northeast Baltimore and gone to a business meeting in the city.

I look around and see my older sister, Terry, who is supervising me for the day. And right beside the court is an elderly man sitting in a lawn chair. But Harold's dad is nowhere in sight. Harold is now playing and crying. Still, he manages to even the set at four-all. Then his dad shows up. Harold stops crying, wakes up, and beats me, 6-4, in the third.

Although he goes on to win the tournament I'm by far his toughest match. I'm encouraged. That could have been me winning the trophy. Pretty soon, it is me. I start winning tournaments left and right. I beat Harold in seven straight boys' 12-and-under finals. That's when his dad packs up the entire family and moves to Miami, Florida.

17

There are no hard feelings about any of it. It's just tennis. That's why they put up a net and keep score. In fact, through the years, we all formed a tight bond. Harold and I traveled together with his dad to out-of-state junior tournaments. We roomed together. We practiced together. We even played some pretty good doubles together. Harold becomes "Chucky" and his dad, Leonard, becomes "The Fox." I'm treated like family.

In May of 1962, when I'm eleven years old, the Fox has my dad send me down to Florida for a tournament. I stay at the Solomon's house in Miami. Harold has three younger siblings—a brother, Mark, and two sisters, Barbara and Shelly. Everyone plays tennis, including the Fox and his wife, Roz. It's the all-American tennis family. Other than my dad, I'm the only tennis player in my family of two older sisters, Eileen and Terry, and a younger brother, Robert.

We all go to the tournament in Miami Gardens—all of the Solomons that is and their newly adopted kid, Steve Krulevitz. Mark and Barbara are playing, too. Our matches are at different times so we don't all arrive together.

I get to the courts for my first-round match about two hours early and have some time to kill. I notice that right next to the tennis facility are some basketball hoops, and some kids are shooting around. I wander over. At one basket, a kid wearing tennis whites is playing with a couple of other kids. *Must be in the tournament*, I think.

"Hey, can I shoot a few with you?" I ask.

"Sure, you playing in the tournament?" the kid in tennis whites asks. I am wearing my tennis whites, too.

"Yeah," I say. "I'm playing later this morning."

"What's your name?" the kid asks me.

"Steve," I say.

"Well, Steve, can you play ball?"

I nod, confidently.

"Good," he says. "I'm Eddie. Now let's play these two bozos for a soda."

We beat the other kids ten baskets to four. Eddie is good. He can shoot. I make a few jump shots off the dribble myself. We're having fun.

"What's your last name?" I ask Eddie.

"Dibbs," he says. "I'm Eddie Dibbs. I live over in Miami Beach."

He gets right back to business and says, "Let's play these guys for five bucks. It's easy money."

We win again. Eddie collects the five dollars. "Here," he

says, handing me three dollars. "You made most of the points. Next time we'll play them for twenty." Then he heads back to the tennis courts.

Chapter 3

Welcome to Miami Beach

In the summer of 1965, I go on what you might call a tear in the boys' 14-and-under division, winning seven strong tournaments in a row along the East Coast, including the Maryland State Juniors, the Mid-Atlantic Conference, and the Eastern Sectional Championships. That last one was particularly big because the tournament was held at the West Side Tennis Club in Forest Hills, New York, which at the time was the site of the United States Open Tennis Championships (now known as the U.S. Open). Today, that tournament is played not far away at Flushing Meadows—Corona Park in Queens, New York.

In late July, I was seeded seventh at the National Championships in the boys' 14-and-under, which was played in Chattanooga, Tennessee. I won my first-round match easily, so when I looked at the draw and saw my next opponent, I said, "Great. Alexander Mayer from Woodmere, New York. What a piece of cake."

Four days earlier, Harold and I had beaten Mayer and his nine-year-old brother, Eugene, in the boys' 14-and-under doubles final of the Eastern Sectional, 8-6, 6-1. The kid could hit, for sure. But he was fat, really fat. And, not surprisingly, didn't move so great.

But when Mayer had me down, 6-2, 3-0, panic set in. This kid wasn't missing a ball. Not only that, he was calling out the score after every point—yeah, even the ones on my serve—which, in addition to the fact that I was getting killed, was pissing me off to no end.

During the changeover at 3-0 in the second set, my buddy Eddie "Fast" Dibbs, who was also playing in the tournament, came over to me and said, "Hey, Vitz," calling me by my tennis nickname, "What's going on?" That's when the panic really set in.

I wanted to win so badly. Getting busted at National in the second round of the boys' 14-and-under would be a crushing blow. I tried to refocus and block out the noise of this kid calling out the score after *every point*. But I was in too deep a hole and went down 6-2, 6-4. Busted in the second round by a kid from Long Island.

"Busted" was a huge word on the junior tour in those days. When you were playing a seeded player, other kids would come up to you and say, "Good luck, bust that guy."

On the other end, if you pulled off a big win over a seed they'd say, "Hey, you really busted that guy."

The big thing was not to get busted yourself. But busted I was. Early rounds can be mentally tough like that, especially at a tournament like National, where there is so much at stake.

In retrospect, though, I didn't have a whole lot to be ashamed of. This kid Mayer might have been playing his first year in the 14's, but he was a whole lot better than I realized. He had finished the previous year ranked eighth in the country in the boys' 12-and-under, demolishing Harold in the Eastern Sectional finals along the way. This year he was the boys' 14-and-under champ of New York.

A couple of years later, in high school, Alex "Sandy" Mayer would run cross-country in the fall and eat only rice for breakfast, lunch, and dinner. He'd lose the extra pounds, win the 1973 National Collegiate Athletic Association (NCAA) Singles Championship as a senior at Stanford, and then he and Gene would become the first—and, as of this writing, only brothers to be ranked in the world's top ten in singles. They'd team together for nine doubles titles, too, including the 1979 French Open. It turned out their father, Alex Sr., was a former Davis Cup player for Hungary and an extremely accomplished teaching pro. He had come over to the States and eventually settled in, of all places, Long Island,

New York.

Even so, my summer had been good enough to get me into the Orange Bowl International Tennis Championships, down in Miami Beach, Florida, one of the most prestigious junior tennis tournaments in the world. That tournament was going to be my redemption.

The Orange Bowl wasn't until December. In the meantime, I decided I could get faster if I dropped a little weight. So I started either skipping lunch or eating very little at school. I was probably the fastest kid in the seventh grade, and I could run down any ball on a tennis court, but I somehow got the idea that I could be faster. I was so competitive. Always had to be the best, not only at tennis but at whatever sport I was playing.

Well, I eventually got rundown, and then picked up the Asian flu. Chills. Fever. Sweats. I was a mess. This was particularly unusual because I was an extremely healthy kid. I was hardly ever sick, and my energy levels were high. I was always moving. But the Asian flu took me down, big time. This flu was no joke. The initial outbreak in 1957 and 1958 killed almost 70,000 people in the United States and at least a million people worldwide, maybe even as many as four million, according to some estimates. This was not something to play around with, by any means.

After about five days, I started feeling better but still had this horrendous cough. Then someone at school told me that Florida is really the place to go after being sick.

Since I was already heading down there for the tournament, I asked my dad, who was a doctor after all, if I could go a little earlier. My family was planning on taking a Christmas trip to Miami Beach anyway. You know. Sun. Beach. Orange Bowl. And a visit with my mom's sister, who lived on Collins Avenue. I talked Casey into letting me, at fourteen, fly down to Florida solo. I don't think kids do that sort of thing as much in today's world. I was an independent kid.

I arrived in Miami on a Thursday. I was staying with my best tennis friend, Eddie Dibbs. Eddie lived directly across the street from Flamingo Park. Perfect location for the Orange Bowl, which was held on the park's clay courts in those days.

Eddie's mom was a doll. Almost as great as my mom. She and Eddie picked me up at Miami International Airport on Friday morning. The Orange Bowl did not start until Monday. So that night, Eddie and I look for something to do. You have to understand one thing about Eddie, even back then, he was fourteen going on thirty-four. You had to be cool around him.

After hitting a few practice balls over at Flamingo Park, I try to be cool, of course, like Eddie, and I ask, "Hey, what's there to do around here on a Friday night? Where's the action?" Big mistake. I mean, I was fourteen years old.

"There's a place up on the beach," Eddie says, reluctantly. "A lot of kids get together on Friday nights. They have a dance or something."

So, being Mister Smarty Pants, I say, "Let's go up there and check it out."

"It can be a little dangerous," Eddie says. "But we can check it out." I'm guessing Eddie agreed to do this because, one, I was staying at his house, and, two, he probably didn't know what to do with me. I had a lot of energy.

After dinner, we start to head out the door. It's already getting kind of dark. Eddie's mom says, in her Brooklyn accent, "Where you boys going?"

The Dibbs family had moved to Florida from Brooklyn, New York. But they never lost their New York accents. Eddie's dad was an auctioneer and one very, very funny guy. Eddie's sister was a few years older and always hanging out with her friends.

Eddie immediately lies to his mom, of course, and says, "We're going up to Washington Avenue, Mom, to get some bagels for breakfast tomorrow and take a walk around." He was, after all, fourteen going on thirty-four.

We actually did pick up a half-dozen bagels on Washington Avenue, so it turned out Eddie hadn't completely lied to his mom after all. Then we headed over to the Miami Beach Recreational Center on Ocean Drive. You weren't allowed to take any food or drink inside, so we stashed the bagels behind the building, on the beach.

Eddie knew just about everyone in the place. It was a good rowdy bunch of kids. We walked in and then down some steps. Surrounding the hardwood dance floor were rows of chairs on all sides. It looked like they probably put on plays and dance recitals in there.

That's when my eyes went straight to a girl sitting in the second row. All by her lonesome self. This girl is a knockout. Drop-dead gorgeous. Blonde hair. Sun-tanned. *I want to meet her*, I think.

"Who's that?" I ask Eddie, looking over at the girl.

Eddie turns to face me and says, "She is with the Cubans. Stay away, that's trouble." But I had to meet her. Never mind that I had no idea what I would do with her anyway. I'd gone to a spin-the-bottle party once.

Eddie goes off to say hi to a friend. So I decide to go over there and sit down right next to her. We're in the second of three rows of folding chairs.

"Hi," I say. "I'm Steve." She doesn't answer. Doesn't look at me. "I'm from Baltimore," I say. Nothing.

Right then, this kid walks over to us in front of the first row of chairs and starts speaking Spanish to the girl, then to me. I don't understand a thing.

"Girlfriend?" the kid finally asks, in broken English, pointing to the blonde. And stupid me says, "Yes" and nods.

Next thing I know the kid leans over, reaches between the chairs, and slaps me really, really hard on the left side of my face with his right hand. It makes a loud clapping sound. Scares the crap out of me. My face starts to sting almost immediately. I become infuriated. I reach out across the chairs, grab him by the shoulders, and coconut his head with mine. Hard. Really hard.

Now it's totally on. He grabs me, and I've still got a hold of him, too. We knock over the chairs and go rolling around on the hardwood floor. The whole thing lasts about forty-five seconds. It's for real. Luckily for me, I had wrestled a season at the Jewish Community Center (JCC) back home. The Bookman and I were the one-two punch. I was pretty good. But not that good. All of a sudden, some big dude has me in a full nelson. Of course, anybody was a big dude to me; I was a little small for my age.

"It's okay, it's okay," I say. "I'm a friend of Eddie Dibbs. Take it easy."

Right up the stairs the big dude and I go, still locked onto me in a full nelson. He drags me into a dark office and orders me to sit down. Seconds later, Eddie comes in. The two of them talk it over, and then the big dude says to me, "You have two minutes to get out of here."

Two minutes is about one minute and forty-five seconds longer than I need. I take off, while Eddie stays behind and continues to try to smooth things over.

Now I'm standing outside the Rec Center on Ocean Drive, waiting for Eddie, anxious to get away from this place as fast as I can. Finally, the door opens…

But it's not Eddie. Instead out comes my new Cuban friend. *I really don't want any more trouble*, I think. That's when I remember the bagels. "You want a bagel?" I say to the kid. He looks at me like I'm crazy. "You want a bagel?" I ask again. No answer.

Now that I was getting a good look at him, I see he couldn't have been any older than fifteen. Also, for some reason, he was looking at me with terror in his eyes. Or maybe it's just that his eyes were still a little glossy from that head-butt I'd given him.

"I have some bagels," I say.

"What?" he finally replies, in broken English.

"Bagels," I say, and I make a motion with my hand up to my mouth and start chewing, like I'm eating a bagel.

"*Dónde*?" he asks. Where? Hey, maybe he really does want one!

"I'll get one for you," I say, jumping at this opportunity to extend a bagel-cum-olive branch and make peace. "They're right back there on the beach!"

That's when Eddie finally comes out and walks over to me. "Forget the bagels. We gotta get out of here," he says.

"What about the bagels?" I ask. "I'll run back there and get them." I was so dumb.

"If you go back there," Eddie says, "this kid will knife you."

Then, at the exact same moment, we both turn to the left and see, in the distance, a group of kids running up the sidewalk toward us. My new Cuban friend leaves my side and starts running toward them, clearly to join forces. Things are moving fast.

"Follow me," says Eddie. "Don't look back.

We tear across Ocean Drive with cars coming toward us

in both directions. I dodge a speeding car, almost getting hit, and then Eddie and I go into a dead sprint. Heavy sprint. Death Sprint. We're running, literally, for our lives. Thankfully, Eddie knows the neighborhood like the back of his hand. We run between houses, across alleys, lawns. Never looking back, not once.

We enter Eddie's house, through the back alley, as usual, run over to the couch that's up against the front window, and get down real quick. We can hear a mob of kids running up and down the street. Looking for us, for sure. We stay down. We dodged a bullet.

Thankfully, after that close call, everything returns to normal. The next day Eddie and I hit some balls on the Flamingo Park tennis courts. On Sunday we shoot some baskets. It is great being in Florida. At 3:00 p.m., the draw is coming out for the Orange Bowl.

We're back at Eddie's house, relaxing. It's quarter to three. "Hey, you want to go over and check the draw?" I ask Eddie.

"You go, Vitz," he says. "Let me know when I play."

It's obvious he wasn't concerned. Eddie was cocky! After all, he was the tournament's top seed and, on top of that, he's playing on his home courts. I'm seeded eighth and also playing in the doubles with Harold. Together we have made it to the doubles finals the last two years of this tournament. This year we're seeded fourth.

So, I walk across the street by myself to check the draw. I'm playing Luis Baraldi from Mexico City on Tuesday. Eddie doesn't play until Wednesday.

I walk back across the street and down the alley toward Eddie's townhouse. We always come in and out the back door. His house is the fourth one on the left. I am feeling much better. My cough is completely gone. It is a beautiful day. Blue, blue sky. Warm sun. Nothing at all like Baltimore in December.

Then I notice a kid on a bike coming toward me. He gets within about five yards of me and suddenly stops. The bike looks too big for him, but he seems to be managing it okay.

"Hey," the kid says to me. "Aren't you the guy the Cubans are looking for?"

I stop and look at him. He's about nine or ten years old at the most.

"I don't think it's me you're talking about," I say.

"Yeah, I'm pretty sure you are the guy that the Cubans are looking for," he says. And, just like that, he pulls out a gun. I have no idea if the gun is real or fake. But it's big. And

32

it definitely looks real. *Very real.*

The kid is standing between the bars of the bike, his feet barely touching the ground, and yet he has perfect balance. "I know you," he says, pointing the gun right at my face.

With a gun pointed at my face, I figure now it would be better to agree with him.

"Yeah, it's me," I say.

"The Cubans are looking everywhere for you," the kid says. "Now get out of here before I shoot you."

I take off in a sprint. I run right past Eddie's back door and down the alley. When I get to the end of the alley, I look back and see the kid on the bike, still watching me. I turn left onto the sidewalk. I'm really scared. I walk around for a couple of blocks before heading back to Eddie's house. Doesn't look like anyone is following me. And there's no sign of the Cubans. This time, I enter straight through Eddie's front door.

"Steve, are you okay?" Eddie's mom asks me. "You look pale."

"I'm fine," I say, "just need some more Florida sun."

When I tell Eddie the story, he laughs and laughs. He thinks it's funny.

Welcome to Miami Beach.

***

Now it's dinner time on Monday night. My last night staying with the Dibbs. My family is coming in from Baltimore for vacation, and I'll be staying with them.

"Let's go up to the deli and get a hotdog with bologna," Eddie says. I'm a little hesitant to go for a stroll in his neighborhood. Rough couple of days.

"Do you think the Cubans will be around?" I ask him. "No way," he says. "They stay down south. We're heading north. They never come up this far. Never."

"How far is the deli?" I ask.

"About five blocks north," Eddie says. "We're safe. Great dog. Come on."

I figure Eddie knows the turf. He's got to play Wednesday, first match in the Orange Bowl. I doubt he's going to take a chance getting jumped tonight. "Okay, let's do it," I say.

Walking to the deli, I suddenly feel like I've been in Miami for a year. Five blocks never seemed so long. "This place has the best dogs with bologna in the world," Eddie says, when we finally get there.

We each get one. I put mustard on mine, and Eddie puts ketchup on his. Everything is cool. We get a couple of Cokes and life is good. We're relaxing, having dinner.

Suddenly, Eddie stands up, grabs his throat and mutters, "It's stuck, it's stuck."

"Very funny," I say, figuring it's a joke.

But then I notice he is turning blue. Seriously, blue. Eddie jumps up on his chair and starts waving his arms around. Now I know he's not kidding. He is in trouble. He's choking. I jump up and grab Eddie around the chest and I lift him up a few inches off the floor. He is heavy as hell.

A piece of bologna shoots out of his mouth onto the floor. I had squeezed his chest so hard when I tried to lift him that I actually did the Heimlich maneuver without even meaning to.

We both sit down, exhausted. Eddie is dripping in sweat, but the color in his face is returning to normal. We look at each other and don't say a thing, just go back to finishing our dogs—mine still with bologna, Eddie's now without—and our sodas.

What a nice, relaxing dinner.

***

Eddie and I both coast into the quarterfinals. Next up I am set to play the number two seed: Jimmy Connors of East St. Louis, Illinois.

The year before, Connors had won the Orange Bowl in the boys' 12-and-under. And guess whom he beat in the finals? Yup, that's right, Alexander Mayer, from Woodmere, New York.

Perfect. Here it was. The match I'd been waiting for. Redemption. I beat Connors, and all is right in my world.

Connors is tough on the court. Eddie says he hits very flat and takes the ball early, right as it comes off the court from the bounce. This does not give a player much time to recover from his shot.

We're playing on court 13, right next to the field where all the American kids who are in the tournament get together to play touch football. Stockton played. Gottfried played. Dibbs played. I played. We all played, except Connors.

My dad is there. And so is Connors' mother, Gloria, and his grandmother, whom we called "Two-Mom." They're all sitting in the bleachers.

I start out playing some great, solid clay court tennis. I'm pumped. Connors takes the first set, 6-3, but I come roaring back and take the second set, 6-4.

Jimmy and I have two contrasting playing styles. Jimmy uses a two-handed backhand while I have a one-handed backhand. On the forehand, Jimmy hits flat and sometimes with sidespin. This allows for the ball to clear the net lower and get to the other side faster. On the other hand, I hit the forehand with topspin and brush up on the ball. This makes the ball hit the court and kick upward. Although topspin slows the ball down and gives your opponent more time to recover, it clears the net more safely. Two very different styles—topspin versus flat.

Jimmy and I also have different playing techniques. Jimmy takes the racquet straight back towards the fence for his forehand and backhand. Conversely, I place the head of the racquet next to my ear and make a circle or backwards letter C on both my forehand and backhand. Maury always told me to keep my wrist slightly "cocked up" on both sides. In doing this, my racquet head points straight up towards the sky. Jimmy's racquet head points straight back to the fence behind him.

Jimmy serves left-handed which can be a big advantage. If you are right-handed, you worry about that. Right-handed players are not used to playing left-handed players. But lefties play and practice against righties all the time. So what really screws up a lefty is playing another lefty. That can get ugly.

The serve of a lefty comes at you from a different angle. It can take a little while to read and adjust to the spin. Jimmy takes the racquet straight up on his serve and uses more of an Eastern Forehand grip.

I serve right-handed and use Continental grip. In order to play with Continental grip you first need to know Eastern Forehand. Eastern Forehand grip (for right-handed players) is when you hold the racquet out in front of you with your left-hand and shake hands with the racquet with your right. From there you move your right hand about a quarter turn to the left for Continental grip. This grip is great for serves, slices, overheads, and volleys. You do not want your wrist "cocked up" though. You have to relax your wrist and be loose. On my serve, I take the racquet straight down past my toes, back towards the fence, and then up toward the sky. I use the same circular motion like on my forehand and backhand.

At 2-1 in the third set, I go to change sides and see Jimmy at the back of the court on the field side, talking to his mom through the fence. I look over at the bleachers for my dad. Then I notice a man and a kid waiting to cross over from court two to our court.

What's going on here? The man looks very official. It turns out there is a good reason: he is an official. He walks up to me and says, "We're going to have someone call the lines in your match." And then walks away, leaving a kid no more than sixteen or seventeen years old in charge at the net, to serve as our line judge. Apparently, Connors' mother and grandmother had convinced the tournament director that I was cheating.

Unbelievable. I wasn't cheating. No way. And they knew it. After that, my concentration was shot. No excuses though. I lost fair and square. Jimmy was just better. He took the third ferocious set, 9-7. Tough loss. Really tough. All I could do was chalk it up to experience. I was still only fourteen years old. Redemption would have to wait.

But, hey, it wasn't all bad. I had learned how to do the Heimlich maneuver and saved the life of my good buddy Eddie Dibbs. Eddie actually wound up winning the tournament, beating Jimmy in the finals in three sets. He won the doubles, too, paired with his usual partner and North Miami Beach friend, Harold Rabinovitz.

I had saved the life of the 1965 Orange Bowl boys' 14-and-under singles and doubles champion. And on top of that, I avoided getting killed myself — twice. Not too shabby.

Chapter 4

The Zoo

In the United States National Lawn Tennis Association (now known as the USTA, the governing body for tennis in the country) I was a flop in the boys' 16-and-under division. I played well on my turf, around Maryland and D.C., and I had some success outside it. But for two years, nationally, I didn't do much.

Now it's late July 1968, and I'm at the Boys' Junior National Tennis Championships in Kalamazoo, Michigan. The National Championships at Kalamazoo (or, the Zoo, as it's known) is hallowed junior tennis ground. It always has been. Kids from every all over the country fly out there to play each other.

It's my first year playing in the boys' 18-and-under. I win my first two matches easily. Third round, I'm up against the sixth seed — Charlie "The Rubber Band Man" Owens.

Charlie Owens from Tuscaloosa, Alabama was a legend

in the South. The first time I ever saw him play was at the Southern Junior tennis tournament at Davidson College in North Carolina in the summer of 1966. There was a huge crowd of kids and parents watching his match from the side of court eight. I walked over with my buddy Harold "Chucky" Solomon.

"Hey, who's playing?" I asked a kid who was watching the match. Without even looking at me, so he didn't miss a shot, the kid said, "Charlie is playing."

I find out the score is 6-0, 4-0, Charlie. He is killing his opponent. Absolutely torturing this kid with drop shots, lobs, angle volleys, and passing shots. It was like a cat playing with a mouse. A really fast cat and a really demoralized mouse.

Down in Tuscaloosa, Charlie had played some organized football. They did a drill with tackling dummies on wrestling mats. After you hit the dummy, you had to drop to the mat and roll, then get up and do it again. Hit the dummy. Hit the mat. Roll. Repeat. Charlie had it down to a T. And he worked it into his tennis game, to spectacular effect.

I saw it firsthand for the first time at that match at Davidson College. In the middle of a point, Charlie ran full speed for a ball, hit it, fell on the court, rolled over two or three times in a tuck, jumped up, and started playing again — and even won the point. The crowd ate it up. From their reaction, it was clear that, while Charlie continued to torture that poor kid on the other side of the net, all the kids and parents had been waiting for the "Rubber Band Man" to roll. It was amazing. He was a legend.

Southern kids like Charlie were far less tense than Northern, East Coast kids. When a Northern kid would turn up in a Southern tournament, Charlie would make that kid feel like a fool. And all the Southern kids loved it. It was a show. I can tell you that for a fact because right there in that tournament at Davidson College, I had a front-row ticket, the best seat — or, really, the worst seat — in the house.

Charlie Owens beat me in singles — twice. Yes, twice. First he humiliated me, 6-1, 6-0, in the round of sixteen (usually the round before the quarterfinals when sixteen players are left is called the "round of sixteen") of the boys' 18-and-under. Three days later, as the sixth seed, I put up a better fight in the boys' 16-and-under finals, but Charlie, the top seed, still beat me handily, 5-7, 6-1, 6-1.

Less than a month later, Charlie and I met again, this time at the Bitsy Grant Invitational in Atlanta. I'd won this tournament the year before in the boys' 14-and-under. This year, in the boys' 16-and-under, I was seeded second. That didn't matter. Top-seeded Charlie thumped me in the finals, 6-3, 6-1. Not only that but in the doubles final, Charlie and his partner, Grover Reid of South Carolina, beat me and Harold, 6-3, 6-2. Charlie capped that 1966 tennis season by winning the Orange Bowl in the boys' 16-and-under. Over the next couple years, I went up against Charlie in a few more southern tournaments, and, sure enough, every result was not pretty.

In the summer of 1968, Charlie was playing some superb tennis. In June, Charlie had won the Interscholastic Championships, a huge junior tournament held at Baylor School in Chattanooga, Tennessee. I lost in the round of sixteen to Roscoe Tanner, 6-2, 6-3. Roscoe was a heck of a player. I'd beaten him handily in the semifinals of that '66 Bitsy Grant tournament, but two years later, he was really starting to come into his own. By the end of the following year, he'd be the top-ranked junior in the country. As a pro, he'd go on to win the Australian Open and lose a five-set Wimbledon final to Björn Borg, reaching a career-high singles ranking of number four in the world.

Roscoe was from Lookout Mountain, Tennessee. At the 1968 Interscholastic Championships, he was not only playing six miles from his hometown, but he was playing on his home courts at Baylor School. He was the captain of the Baylor School tennis team. That didn't matter though. In the quarterfinals, Charlie, his frequent doubles partner on the junior circuit that year, completely demolished him on his own courts, 6-2, 6-1. A few weeks later, in early July, Charlie lost in the finals of the USNLTA Junior Clay Court tournament, held at the Municipal Tennis Center in Louisville, Kentucky.

Charlie ruled the South. He was king. At any tournament in the South, he was in guys' heads, big time. Even the heads of other guys from the South. Even his doubles partner, it turned out.

So here we were, just two months after Charlie walloped the guy who walloped me at the Interscholastic Championships. Third round of National. Charlie, a member of the Junior Davis Cup team that year, headed to the University of Florida, a top-level college tennis program, in the fall. The King of the South has come to conquer the North. July 31, 1968 — Charlie's 18th birthday.

Playing an opponent whom you've played against in the past but never beaten is a tough mental hurdle to get over. First, you analyze what went wrong. Then, you obsess over what you need to do differently. You can really psyche yourself out.

What game plan should I use? I've tried just about everything. Everything, in this case, except for the Mirrors Strategy. The Mirrors Strategy was something I made up solely for this match against Charlie. Here is how it worked: If Charlie hits crosscourt, I hit crosscourt. If Charlie drop shots me, I drop shot back. If Charlie serves and volleys, I serve and volley. I decided to go with this strategy and try to get in his head a little bit. Psyche him out.

Our match is on one of the show courts. Right in front of the stands. The first set is tight. I'm hanging in and playing well. I know Charlie is trying to make it a clay court match on fairly fast Kalamazoo hard courts. And, frankly, it's working pretty well for him.

At six-all, 30-all, on my serve, we have a make-or-break kind of rally. A battle of the wills. I hit a really good forehand crosscourt. Charlie takes off like a bat out of hell. He hits a forehand down the line on a full run and does one of his patented Rubber Band Man rolls. His shot lands in for a winner. The crowd erupts. Great point. Incredible shot. But this isn't soft Southern dirt we're playing on. It's hard, hard Michigan cement. I can still, to this day, remember the sound of Charlie's body hitting the court. Not good. On the next point, during the rally, I sense that something is not right with the Rubber Band Man. That was a very hard roll. Maybe he's a little shook up.

Honestly, how could he not have been? He had just chased down a ball on a full sprint, thrown himself down on a concrete tennis court, and then rolled over three times like a log. I can tell you that particular maneuver definitely wasn't part of the Mirror Strategy. All these thoughts give me confidence. I believe Charlie is in trouble, and my confidence grows. I win the first set 9-7 and then the second set, 7-5. Gutted it out.

I'm in the round of sixteen and feeling good. It's a huge confidence booster beating Charlie Owens. That boost doesn't last long, however, because in the next round I was scheduled to play Mac Claflin, the ninth seed. Claflin was from Coral Gables, Florida. I'd seen him play before, and the guy was unreal. In 1962, he won the inaugural boys' 12 and under title at the Orange Bowl. At fourteen, Claflin was serving and volleying on every first and second serve. He destroyed everyone in Chattanooga, Tennessee at the 1964 boys' 14-and-under National Championships even winning his quarterfinal match 6-0, 6-0. The following year, still a couple months shy of his 15th birthday, Claflin made it to the semifinals of the boys' 16-and-under at Kalamazoo. In December, he won the Orange Bowl boys' 16-and-under singles title.

Claflin was a can't-miss prodigy. What chance did I have? Beating Charlie was one thing. I'd played him before, several times. I knew his game. I'd only seen Claflin play. And what

I had seen did little to instill any confidence in me.

The morning of the match I hit some balls with Harold Solomon, who was seeded fourth in the boys' 16-and-under. The Fox was there too, of course, up from Florida. He'd actually come up a few days late because of business commitments.

"Hey, Steve, come over here for a minute," the Fox says to me, as I come off the court. He was standing in the parking lot right next to the courts, leaning against a black Cadillac, his rental car for the tournament. The Fox was small in stature—like Harold and, to a lesser extent, me too for that matter—but a giant in business. He had done very well for himself. The Fox was one smart cookie. He had given me some nice tips in the past so I knew he had something important to say.

Harold was off on another court, hitting some more balls with Brian Gottfried, who had just shown up. Gottfried was also playing in the boys' 16-and-under. He was a frequent opponent and friend of Harold's in Florida. Gottfried went on to have a stellar career in the pros, winning 25 singles titles and 54 doubles titles, and reaching the French Open final. His highest singles ranking was number three in the world.

Now, it's just me and the Fox. He wants to talk. I want to listen. The conversation we had changes my life.

"How you feeling, kid?" the Fox asks me, as I walk over to him.

"Good," I say.

The Fox starts right on me in the Fox way. The clever way. "The way I see it, kid, you're not juicing the ball enough," the Fox says.

"I'm not what?" I ask, sheepishly.

"You're not juicing it!" he says. "You got to juice to ball. It's brutal out there, so you got to juice it."

Brutal. Everything was brutal. That was his favorite word, by far. The boys' 18-and-under National Championships was brutal. Harold's match at the Western Championships in Springfield, Ohio was brutal. The Davis Cup match between the United States and Australia was brutal. Everything was brutal. I loved it.

"I have to start juicing the ball," I say. "What does that mean?"

"Sure thing," says the Fox. "Just see the ball and juice it. Smack it. Go for it. I want you to juice every ball that comes to you."

I could feel the Fox's confidence in me.

"You play Claflin this afternoon. Don't' think. Just juice

it. Juice every ball," the Fox says.

"Okay, Fox," I say. "I'll juice every ball."

"Atta boy," he says.

I beat Claflin, 6-4, 6-4. I busted him. Right after the match, the Fox walks up to me. I'm waiting for him to say, "You really juiced it out there." But, instead, with a big smile on his face, he says, "Brutal. That was brutal."

I laugh and say, "Yes it was, it really was."

I make it to the quarterfinals and lose to a kid from Southern California. But this tournament has already been a huge breakthrough for me. Collegiate tennis is around the corner and college coaches are now interested in me. I've made a name for myself.

By the end of the following year, I'm ranked seventh nationally in the boys' 18-and-under, my highest ranking as a junior. The next summer, I'm named to the Junior Davis Cup team. All that might never have happened if the Fox hadn't given me that advice at the Zoo. So a big thank you to the Fox. It's brutal out there.

Chapter 5

Don't Budge

"Steve. It's Arthur Kramer from the Suburban Club. I haven't seen you for a few years. How are you?"

The Suburban Club in Baltimore has a rich tennis tradition, along with a couple of nice golf courses and swimming pools. It's predominantly Jewish. When I was five years old, my family moved up Park Heights Avenue closer to Pikesville, a suburb just outside the city. Growing up, I was close enough to walk over to the Suburban Club from my house. Back then, they hosted a big men's city tournament. I played in it for the first time when I was fourteen and made it to the quarterfinals.

Don Candy was the head pro at the Suburban Club. You may have heard of him. Don is an Aussie who played on the amateur tour in the 1950s. He won the doubles title at the French Open and made it to the doubles finals of the Australian and U.S. Opens. He was Pam Shriver's coach on the pro tour for years. Don is a swell guy, and we hit it off pretty well.

After my quarterfinal showing, Don invites me to come back anytime I wanted and hit balls with the club members. The Suburban Club puts the courts and atmosphere at Druid Hill Park to shame. But the Druid Hill Park courts were my home courts. I practiced every day on those red clay courts. That's right, red clay, with white painted lines and a big roller and huge comb-like brushes to sweep them. The whole deal. That's where I grew up as a tennis player. The red clay would get on your socks and never come out. Playing at Suburban was like heaven to a public park player.

In June 1969 when I'm eighteen years old, I graduate from the Park School of Baltimore, a private school just north of the city line. What a great four years.

Park School's athletic teams are good. We play hard and we are hungry to win. As a small school, we don't have a football team and most kids play two or three sports during the school year. I play four.

Spring is always busy for me. Tennis matches on Mondays and Wednesdays. Lacrosse games Tuesdays and Fridays. Plus school work. Heaven on Earth is the best way to describe it. Tight-knit teammates. Tight-knit classmates. We were all in this together.

What could be better than playing on your high school varsity soccer, basketball, lacrosse, and tennis teams, while also receiving a first class education, especially if you loved sports the way my dad and I did? We were big fans — Baltimore Orioles: Brooks Robinson, Jim Palmer, and the Baltimore Colts: Johnny Unitas, Raymond Berry.

I remember December 28, 1958 like it was yesterday. I'm seven years old and freezing behind a pole with my dad in Yankee Stadium. Baltimore Colts versus New York Giants. The greatest game ever played. I watch as Unitas drives us down 71 yards in two minutes and five seconds to set up a tying field goal. The Baltimore Colts beat the New York Giants in sudden-death overtime. We are the 1958 World Champions.

The summer after graduation, I win the Men's City Championships, a tournament that is held at the Suburban Club. A few days later I receive a call from Arthur Kramer, who is a member of Suburban Club. "Hey, Steve," Arthur says. "What are you doing next Saturday afternoon? I'm having a few people over to the house. I have a beautiful court, and I was wondering if you could stop by and hit some balls with Ramiro."

"Ramiro?" I ask.

"Yes, Ramiro Benavides, from Bolivia. He's going on the

pro tour," Arthur says. That kicked up my interest about three notches.

A year earlier, in 1968, the "Open era" of tennis had begun. Professional tennis players would now compete alongside amateurs in the world's most prestigious tournaments, including the four Grand Slams—the Australian Open, the French Open, Wimbledon, and the U.S. Open. This made the pro tour even more enticing to a young tennis player. Rod Laver seemed to be pretty pleased about it, too.

At the time of my phone conversation with Arthur, the legendary Aussie had already won the Australian and French Opens that year. He'd go on to win Wimbledon and the U.S. Open. All four major titles, in one calendar year: the Grand Slam. He'd done it before, in 1962, as an amateur, and is still, to this day, the only man to do it twice.

Arthur, meanwhile, went on, "I thought you could play a set with Ramiro. Don Budge is coming over, too. We're going to have lunch. It would be great to have you."

Well, speaking of the Grand Slam, Budge invented the Grand Slam. He was the first guy to do it, in 1938. The Australian, French, Wimbledon, and U.S. Open, all in one year. Don Budge—a legend! And he was going to be at Arthur Kramer's on Saturday.

I knew Budge had a tennis camp at McDonogh School, which at the time was an all-boys military cadet prep school, also not far over the city line. That season, Park had played McDonogh in basketball and won. I was the starting point guard on the varsity team. In fact, we'd gone undefeated that year and won our conference.

"Sure, Arthur," I say, "I can make it."

Saturday rolls around. It's 11:45 a.m., and I'm standing in the shade by the tennis court at Arthur Kramer's house. Arthur sees me and yells out, "Steve, over here!" He's standing in the doorway of a tennis-style pool house about twenty yards from the court. Nice set up. I walk over to the house. Arthur steps out with a big grin.

"Hi, Steve," Arthur says. "Welcome." We shake hands.

"Steve, I want you to meet someone," says Arthur. "Don, this is Steve Krulevitz." I shake his hand. Man, I just shook Don Budge's hand. His hand is enormous.

"I'm going to hit a few balls with Ramiro," I say eagerly to Budge, who is in his mid-fifties. "If you see anything in my game that needs improvement, could you tell me? I want to play on the pro tour like Ramiro one day." Budge nods and smiles a bit but doesn't say anything.

Ramiro shows up. He's about five years older than I am

and little. We start to hit. Then people start arriving, right and left. It's a big party. Ramiro and I are the entertainment, I guess.

Ramiro and I decide to play a couple of sets. Right off the bat, I can see he's trying hard. Too hard for a party atmosphere. I understand it though. He's trying to impress the spectators.

The food shows up. I can hear the glasses clinking in the house. It's getting hot on the court. They're drinking and eating in the house.

We change sides every third game and I glance into the house, hoping Budge will come out. I can still hear the laughing and talking and those cocktail glasses jingling.

I find out later through the Jewish grapevine that ten Suburban Club members had chipped in $1,000 each so Ramiro could go on the pro tour.

At 6-3, 5-2, me, I realize two things very clearly. One, Don Budge isn't setting foot out of that house for all the tea in China. The only movements he's made the entire hour and a half Ramiro and I have been on the court are two steps to the bar and three steps to the buffet. And two, Ramiro is going to have a tough time on the tour.

We stop after I win the next game and the second set.

Arthur comes out of the house and says, "That was great." I doubt he saw more than two points.

"Come on in and grab some food," he says. "We have plenty. Then we'll do the presentation." Which means the check will be delivered to Ramiro and everyone will be happy.

"Thanks, Arthur," I say. "Be there in a minute."

Arthur and Ramiro walk off together toward the pool house. I can't go in there. I split, quickly. The ride home is depressing.

Chapter 6

Motor Learning Skills

After practice one afternoon, Glenn Bassett, the University of California, Los Angeles, Head Varsity Tennis Coach, says to me, "Hey, Steve, one day soon before practice, check with the guidance counselor up in the Athletic Office over in Pauley."

"Pauley" was Pauley Pavilion, home of the NCAA Champion basketball team coached by John Wooden. I had arrived on campus right in the heart of the UCLA basketball team's mid-1960s to mid-1970s dominance. From 1967 to 1973, the team won seven straight national titles. In the twelve years between 1964 and 1975, they won the title a total of ten times. UCLA was a good place to be in those days if you were a basketball fan. Heck, it was a good place to be if you were a sports fan. UCLA was just a good, beautiful place to be period, regardless of whether you loved college sports, music or surfing or just being alive and breathing. The weather. The beach. The mountains. Beautiful women. Jock heaven. I loved it.

"Sure, Coach," I say.

"What time is your flight on Friday?" Coach Bassett asks.

"My flight leaves at 11:00 a.m.," I say."

"Okay," Coach says, "don't forget to check in at Pauley when you get back."

How would you like to hit with Coach Glenn Bassett every Wednesday all year long from 9:00 a.m. to 10:00 a.m. at UCLA? Those around you shape who you are and who you become. How would you like to be around a guy who won the National Collegiate Athletic Association (NCAA) tennis title not only as a player but also as Assistant Coach and Head Coach? How about this for a coaching record: 592-92-2, thirteen Conference titles, seven NCAA team championships (in 1970, 1971, 1975, 1976, 1979, 1982, and 1984), three NCAA singles championships, four NCAA doubles team championships, forty-nine All Americans, UCLA Tennis Hall of Fame, International Tennis Collegiate Tennis Hall of Fame, Southern California Tennis Association Hall of Fame, and Santa Monica College Sports Hall of Fame. Not a bad guy to hang around and pick up a few pointers. And don't forget about his two books—Tennis Today and Tennis: the Bassett System.

"Wheels" was Coach's nickname for me. "I love your wheels and the way you cover the court," Coach would say to me. "I've never seen anyone faster." Coming from Coach, this means the world to you.

"Take a break. "Be sure not to practice too much on the weekends." Imagine a college coach telling one of his starting players this today. Kids over-train at all levels and in all sports. Imagine practicing for only two hours. That's it. But those two hours are intense. Never resting. You go all out. It builds you up and teaches you discipline, concentration, and to believe in yourself. If Coach Basset believes in you that is all that matters at UCLA. These were lessons stored for later in life. Just ask any of those 49 All Americans.

***

It's March 1974, and I am qualifying at the American Airlines Tennis Games. It's a one hour flight to Tucson, Arizona. An easy pop. I get there at noon, take a shuttle to the players' hotel, check-in, and then get a ride to the tournament site to practice.

Now it's two o'clock in the afternoon and hot. The sun seems more intense than in California. No one is around. Qualifying starts at nine o'clock Saturday morning. Main draw at ten o'clock Monday morning.

I notice a male hitting with a female on court four at the American Airlines tournament site. *I've seen that player before*, I think. Then, I remember, that's Vijay Amritraj. Vijay and the female player walk towards the net and shake hands. I walk over to court four. They are friendly and polite.

"I'm Vijay and this is Margaret," Vijay says to me.

"I'm Steve," I say.

I immediately recognize the female player as Margaret Court. She is the best female player in the world. I have been following tennis religiously since I was eleven when my dad got me a subscription to World Tennis Magazine. Margaret Court was a hero to me. She won all four Grand Slam titles in 1970 — the Australian, French, Wimbledon, and U.S. Open. She won seven Australian Championships in a row in the '60s. In 1962, she won the French Open, Wimbledon, and the U.S. Open. I know she was also a great doubles player, and I should add, mixed doubles player. Margaret won singles, doubles, and mixed doubles at all four Grand Slam tournaments, twice. Totaling 24 Grand Slam singles, 19 Grand Slam doubles, and 19 Grand Mixed doubles titles. That is 62 titles she would claim before retiring from the sport in 1977.

"Nice to meet you," I say to Margaret. "I saw you practicing a few times at UCLA. I'm on the team there. Congratulations on all your success."

"My entire family moved to Los Angeles a few months ago," Vijay says.

"That's great," I tell him.

"We'll have to practice together sometime soon," Vijay says. "But today I have had plenty. Margaret has worn me out."

Margaret jumps in and says, "I'll hit with you Steve. But only for one hour."

"Sure," I say.

We both start out at the service line for volleys. Man, can she volley. Crisp, firm, rapid fire. I am struggling a bit to keep up. She is at the service line, and I am at the service line: back and forth with pace. Fifteen minutes and I am sweating profusely but loving it. Totally.

Margaret says, "I'll hit crosscourt, and you go down the line."

This is a tough drill. Have to really hustle. After ten minutes I am calling uncle. "Let's grab a drink," I say.

My shirt is soaked. I sit in the chair by the court.

Margaret stands at the net.

"Wish I could play doubles with you at this tournament," I say.

She laughs.

"I mean it," I say, "your volleys are incredible."

"Thank you, Steve. But I'm just starting to get back into it after the baby. I need to do a lot of fitness. How about if I hit down the line and you go crosscourt?"

"With pleasure, Mrs. Court."

One hour later, I'm beat. I'm sure she could have played another hour.

"Thanks for the hit, Steve. Good luck in the tournament."

"Good luck to you too. See you around."

Off she went. The Legendary Margaret Smith Court. What a class act. The qualifying did not go great, but the hit with Margaret Court certainly did.

A week later, I'm back at UCLA in the Athletic Office at Pauley Pavilion. "Well, Steve," my guidance counselor says, "we love having you here in Westwood, however, we don't want you here forever."

Leave it to a guidance counselor to bring reality crashing back down.

"I looked over your transcripts, and you've fulfilled some important credits toward a degree in Physical Education," Bill continues. "And you're doing very well in that major."

Not knowing what to major in, I had decided on Physical Education. I thought it would be easy. I was carrying a 3.0 grade point average at the time.

"You know," Bill says, "UCLA is going to do away with Physical Education altogether. We're changing the name of that major to Kinesiology."

"Kinesi-what?" I ask.

"Kinesiology," he says, and hands me a printout of all the kinesiology classes, the corresponding times, and teachers. A complete schedule. "In two and a half years, or less, you will have a bachelor's of science degree in Kinesiology from UCLA. I spent a lot of time on this, Steve," Bill tells me.

I look at the paper. Chemistry. Exercise physiology. Anatomy, with a lab. Physics. Whew. This looks rough. Kinesiology — the study of movement. I've never heard of it.

Bill stood in sharp contrast to my high school guidance counselor Richard Peyton at the Park School. In our final meeting together, he told me to forget about college. "You should go to a vocational school and learn a trade," he said. Huge vote of confidence in my abilities. Although, based on some of my grades back then, he might have had reason to say that. I wasn't exactly crushing the books. I cared about sports too much. I got all A's in history. Loved it. Science and

English were okay. I didn't care so much for Algebra or Geometry.

In early 1974, during my last semester at UCLA, I'm riding a 3.2 grade point average, thank you very much. Not bad for a kid who probably shouldn't even have gone to college. UCLA's tennis team had the highest GPA of any varsity sport. We had some smart kids on the team: Jeff Austin, Brian Teacher, and Mike and Bob Kreiss. Very intelligent guys. And we had one incredible, world-class coach.

To graduate, all I need to do is pass Dr. Cratty's Motor Learning Skills class. There's only one problem. One big problem. The midterm. I bomb it. Totally. This class is kicking my butt. I couldn't get the material. Only thing to do is get help. I'm sure Dr. Cratty has to know a graduate student who can help me. I'm desperate.

I hear that Dr. Cratty is just a wee bit standoffish. His personal contact with his students range from "very little" to "zero." When the midterm grades come out, I go into a semi-panic. After class, I approach Dr. Cratty at his desk. "Dr. Cratty," I say. He doesn't look up from the papers and notes on his desk. "Dr. Cratty," I say again. Still no response. I'm the only student at his desk. Everyone else is filing out of the classroom.

"Dr. Cratty, my name is Steve Krulevitz," I say. "I'm on the tennis team here at UCLA. Last year, I was All-American, and I'm thinking about going on the pro tour after I graduate."

Of course, I was more than thinking about it. I had been working toward this goal for as long as I can remember. Ever since I beat Mac Claflin and Charlie Owens at National.

"I'm taking your class pass-fail," I say. "If I pass, I'll have enough credits to graduate. I don't think I did very well on the midterm." This of course was an understatement.

Dr. Cratty is still not looking at me. He is still looking down at his desk. Then out of the blue, and without even looking at me, he says, "Do you play racquetball?" *What kind of question is that*, I think.

"I've played some," I say.

"Good," he says. "Meet me Thursday at two o'clock in the men's gym." And he gets up and walks away. Still hasn't looked at me, not even once.

Thursday at 2:00 p.m. sharp I'm standing in the men's gym and here comes Dr. Cratty with a couple of racquets, two pairs of goggles, and a racquetball.

"Let's go," he says. "Follow me."

Yeah, he is looking at me now. Still not too friendly. But it seems like a good sign. We go up the stairs, into the court. For one hour we kill each other. Fast, furious game of racquetball. We're soaked. Completely. Great workout.

Afterwards, we sit outside the court by the water fountain. "Steve, I enjoyed that," Dr. Cratty says, "you're pretty good. I'll see you next Thursday." And off he goes with my racquet and goggles.

Every Thursday after that, for the rest of the semester, same scenario. Soaked. And no answer about motor learning class. Still not much conversation between us. Great racquetball games though.

Now it's mid-March. The morning of the final arrives. I take it. The next afternoon, I approach Dr. Cratty's desk, again. "Dr. Cratty," I say, "I'm heading back East in two days. Then off to Spain."

He looks up at me. "I have your blue book right here," he says. And he holds it up. "Let me take a quick look," he says as he opens to the first page. He flips through the book for a minute or two and then says, "This looks good." And gives me a smile.

One week later, Casey is walking down the hall to my childhood bedroom back home. He is holding my graduation

present in his hand, a United Airlines plane ticket to Madrid.
The journey begins.

Chapter 7

Gladiators Do Battle

To get into the main draw of the 1974 Italian Open, I had to win three qualifying matches. I did it without dropping a set. In the final match, I beat this Italian guy, Sergio Palmieri. He was wearing some fine-looking tennis clothes: Sergio Tacchini. Nice-looking gear. Italians have style. I'm still wearing the Wilson shorts and shirts I bought at the Westwood Sporting Goods store in Los Angeles from my good friend Shelby Johns.

Sergio is a very friendly opponent. After the match, he smiles and says to me, "Do you want to wear some of these Tacchini clothes in your first-round match?"

"I would love to," I say.

It's a Sunday afternoon in late May. The tournament starts the next morning. "Where will you be around five o'clock today?" he asks me. I am definitely not going back to my hotel, even though it is near Rome's legendary Spanish

Steps. It isn't very...um...nice. The shower in the tiny bathroom in my room has no door, no curtain, nothing, so the water runs into the room if I shower for more than a minute. It isn't pretty. On the other hand, you do get a continental breakfast. Blood-red orange juice, a cup of coffee, and a hard roll with butter and jam.

"I'll be around the players' lounge," I tell Sergio.

"I'm coming back at five o'clock. Will you definitely be here?" he asks.

"Sure, sure. I'll see you then," I say.

Years later, Sergio would become John McEnroe's agent. So I guess he was already working the deals back then.

At five o'clock, two full bags of Tacchini gear arrive at the players' lounge. Shirts, shorts, tracksuits, socks, vests, bags. Man, this stuff is nice. I'm in heaven.

The Italian Open is the second biggest clay court tournament on the planet. Right behind the French Open in Paris, which is played soon after. The Italian Open is held at the Foro Italico, a sports complex originally known as the Foro Mussolini. Yes, that's Mussolini.

This tournament has tradition. It also has been the setting for some crazy scenes through the years. Usually involving the crowd. It's the Colosseum of tennis. Where the gladiators do battle.

My first-round opponent is Juan Gisbert, a big-time clay court player and Davis Cup stalwart from Spain. Even though he recently turned thirty-two, Gisbert is definitely still kicking. In April, he made it to both the singles and doubles finals at a hard court event in Tokyo, losing the singles in three sets to thirty-five year old Rod Laver. In the week leading up to the Italian, he'd team up with Ilie Nastase to win the doubles at the prestigious British Hard Court Championships in Bournemouth, England, which is played on clay courts at the West Hants Club. (What American tennis has long considered to be "clay courts," our European counterparts termed "hard courts.") This could be a big international win for me.

I'm nervous at the start of the match. I'm looking really sharp in my brand-new Sergio Tacchini gear, but my game is off. I'm down 5-2 in the opening set. I'm letting a great opportunity slip away. I've come too far now, I say to myself during the changeover. As a kid I used to dream about the Italian and French Open, looking at the pictures in World Tennis Magazine. Now I'm here, on court four and I have to fight harder. I have to prove I belong. I have to dig deeper. Gisbert is robbing me of my dream: doing well at the Italian Open, winning at Foro Italico.

A year from then, Gisbert and his Davis Cup teammate Manuel Orantes would make it to the doubles semifinals of the French Open. And then, the following year, they'd do it again. After being up 5-2 in the first round of the 1974 Italian Open, Gisbert only wins two more games the rest of the match. I don't miss a ball. Total concentration. 7-5, 6-2.

Monday night at 11:00 p.m., I can't sleep. Too pumped. My next match is not until Wednesday. So I decide to go for a run. I head out in the back streets. It's quiet. No cars. No buses running. I'm running through the streets of Rome. It's surreal. Euphoric.

On Wednesday, in the second round, I steamroll Raul Ramirez from Mexico, the tournament's fifteenth seed, 6-0, 6-2. Tomorrow is Thursday, May 30, 1974, my twenty-third birthday.

After the match against Ramirez, I'm signing a few autographs when I look up into the stands and see a familiar face. "Hey, Solly!" I shout. No, it's not the Solly we all know. It's not Harold Solomon. It's Sol Goldman.

Sol Goldman is a friend of Eddie Dibbs' from Miami. Solly is in his seventies. He's in Rome to watch the tennis and hang with Eddie, who's the thirteenth seed in the tournament.

"Solly, when did you get here?" I ask. Solly and Eddie

71

have been friends for years. Ever since the day at Flamingo Park when the elder spotted the younger on the next court over and got dollar signs in his eyes.

Sol Goldman played a decent doubles game. Nothing special. But he had a great eye for two very complementary things: tennis talent and hustling doubles matches. He and Eddie hustled every tennis player in Miami Beach. I saw it with my own eyes. They would handicap a set. Give some suckers a 3-0 lead and then play it out. They made quite the team: Eddie was thirteen; Solly was in his late sixties. After winning the set, 7-5, and splitting a hundred bucks, they'd offer to play another set. This time with a 4-0 handicap. Double the bet. They'd beat the guys, 7-5, again. Eddie made a lot of pocket money this way as a kid.

"How long you been on the continent?" Solly shouts down to me.

"This is my ninth week, Solly," I say.

I'd taken off for Europe after finishing my last exam at UCLA. I spent one month in Barcelona alone, eating every single night at Los Caracoles, off the Ramblas, bunking in a hostel with the bathroom and shower down the hall. I read the book Papillon, which had been made into a film starring Steve McQueen and Dustin Hoffman, and released in theaters the year before. I liked it. McQueen had total focus—first to stay alive and second to escape. Being on the tour, on and off the court, requires focus and discipline. Train like a boxer, think like the Queen. After playing some in Madrid I caught the train to Toulouse. Everyone travels the rails in Europe.

Another tourney and then another train to Nice. South of France. Pretty sweet. Flew to Piza, Italy, and caught a bus to Florence. Everyone there thought I was from Yugoslavia — "Franulovic, as in Zelko," "Niki Pilić," and "Steve Krulevitz." I was one of only two Americans in the draw; the other was my old college teammate Bobby Kreiss. We played doubles together. I hopped on a train and played a couple of tournaments in Germany. Then I flew from Hamburg to Rome. Now, I'm in the round of sixteen at the Italian Open.

In 1974, the United States has some darn good tennis players. World number two Jimmy Connors — yeah, that same kid from the 1965 Orange Bowl — isn't playing in Rome because he'd been banned. Earlier that year, he signed a contract to play in the new professional league, World Team Tennis. As it happened, the team he signed with was the Baltimore Banners, coached by my old friend Don Candy. The old guard in tennis didn't appreciate the competition from this rival league.

In February of 1974, the president of the French Tennis Federation announced that players under contract with

World Team Tennis would be denied entry into all tournaments held in his country, including the French Open. The Italian, West German, Swedish, and Eastern European federations subsequently followed suit. A week before the Italian Open, the Italian Federation reaffirmed that Connors was really banned from the tournament. It was tough luck for Jimmy. He had already won that year's Australian Open, and would go on to win Wimbledon and the U.S. Open, too—but not the French Open.

No Grand Slam for Jimmy that year. He would have been the first guy since Laver in '69 to do it. He never really came close again, in fact, he never won the French Open, but only made it four times to the semifinals.

Connors—on his way to claiming the number one ranking that summer, despite all his bans—is out. But Eddie Dibbs, Harold Solomon, Stan Smith, Brian Gottfried, Marty Riessen, Tom Gorman, and Roscoe Tanner are in. These guys are phenomenal tennis players.

A funny and unusual thing happens on that Wednesday after I beat Ramirez in the second round. By nightfall, all the big-name Italians are out of the draw—Adriano Panatta, the fifth seed, Paolo Bertolucci, the seventh seed, and rising star Corrado Barazzutti, the '71 French Open Junior Champion. There's only one Italian left in the draw: Antonio Zugarelli.

And guess who's playing him in the round of sixteen? That's right, me. Word gets out fast. Stadium court. Thursday. Not before 4:00 p.m. Steve Krulevitz, USA vs. Antonio Zugarelli, ITALIA, for a spot in the quarterfinals of the Italian Open.

Now the Italian tournament officials are all over me. "Where are you staying? Would you like to move to the tournament hotel? We can take care of your room for you. The best chef in Rome is cooking for the players in the dining area. Here's two meal tickets for you and a friend."

"I'm fine," I say, with a smile. "*Grazie.*"

We're the last match of the day on Thursday. By the time we step on the court, there are only three Americans left in the draw: Smith, the fourth seed, Gottfried, the fourteenth seed (they're set to meet in the quarterfinals), and one other guy. A qualifier. Unseeded.

Stadium court at the 1974 Italian Open seats 5,000 spectators. For that match, Krulevitz vs. Zugarelli, 4,998 of them are rabid, soccer-style tennis fans. The other two are Eddie Dibbs and Harold Solomon.

The chant begins immediately after the great Argentine, Guillermo Vilas—just beginning to hit his stride in his breakout year—dispatches his third-round opponent, Karl

Meiler of West Germany, on Center court. You can hear the chants under the tunnel. Back into the locker room — "ZUGGY! ZUGGY! ZUGGY!"

It's loud. Very loud. I'm in the locker room, sitting there, listening to it, thinking to myself, It's the Roman Colosseum out there! — feeling like I'm about to be thrown to the lions — 4,998 of them. I'm also thinking that I can't let Zugarelli get into the match. The crowd will be tough to overcome. I've got to silence the crowd. Right off the bat. Got to get ahead. And hold it.

The match is announced on the loudspeaker in the stadium. Krulevitz and Zugarelli. The crowd goes nuts. Ape. We walk through the tunnel, to the court, and into the sunshine. The crowd breaks into the "ZUGGY" chant. The stadium is full to capacity. I see Eddie and Harold sitting in the players' section of the stands behind the far baseline. The atmosphere is electric. The crowd is loud. We stand at the net for pictures. It's like a final.

We start to warm up. The crowd is really into it. Still chanting through the warm-up. It's incredible. It's like a Davis Cup match. There is heavy nationalism in these European countries. The umpire makes no effort to silence the crowd. Why would he? He's Italian. He has to live in Italy after this match.

I know they're trying to get to me. Unnerve me. But, in reality, they're psyching me up, not out—and, unwittingly, putting a lot of pressure on Zugarelli. He's probably thinking, I'm going to be ruined here in Italy if I don't beat this qualifier. Meanwhile, I'm thinking, just relax. Move your feet. Watch the ball. Don't think. Juice it.

Zugarelli feels the pressure. The American wins the first set, 6-2. The Italian crowd is silenced. But they're smart. They sense Zuggy is down. He needs help. So they ramp up the chants. In between games and during the entire changeovers. Nonstop. The umpire can't silence them. It's maddening. I try to stay cool, but it's not easy. I'm losing my focus. Zuggy is playing better, and my level starts to drop.

It's a gladiator fight. Now it's to the death. Dibbs and Solomon are enjoying this scene. I know it. I'm hanging in, barely. It's mental. Three rounds of qualifying just to get into the draw. Beat a former French Open finalist and top 20 player from Spain, where they're basically reared on the red clay, Gisbert. I knocked off another guy, the 1973 singles runner-up at the NCAA Championships, Ramirez, from the University of Southern California (he'd actually beaten me in the round sixteen of in that NCAA tournament). I'm one set away from the quarterfinals of the Italian Open. The ball is coming a little faster now, and my timing is a bit off. That's tennis.

I come close to losing the second set at 5-4 down and then again at 6-5 down. A couple of points from losing the set in both games. Somehow I make it to a tiebreaker. I'm hanging in there… barely. The momentum is switching. The crowd is wild now. The umpire has zero control. I don't make a move to ask him to quiet anyone. There's no way he'll succeed. Things are completely out of control. Plus, if I complain, the crowd and Zugarelli will see that they're getting to me. This will give Zugarelli confidence. Don't make any moves, I tell myself. Take your time. Go to the towel. Slow down.

The umpire announces the tiebreaker. This is it. Zugarelli goes up 5-3. He's two points from evening the match. I have to fight harder. A third set would not be pretty. I've got to put everything into these next few points. I serve a bomb. I'm thinking it might have hit the line. Zuggy gets his racket on it but can't do anything with it. The service linesman calls the serve out. I walk two steps forward, looking at the mark. Then I turn, and my eyes meet the umpire's.

Before I continue, there's something you really should know, for context. The day before, in his second-round match, Zugarelli had played Jan Kodes of Czechoslovakia, the second seed and reigning Wimbledon Champion. In the deciding third set, serving at 4-5, 30-all, Kodes hit a volley on the line for a winner. Or what he—and, apparently, everyone else in the stadium, including Zugarelli, the linesmen, and the chair umpire—thought was a volley on the line for a winner. The tournament referee, an Italian by the name of Michele Brunetti, overruled the call, awarding the point to Zugarelli, giving him a match point. Kodes lost it. Completely. He and Brunetti argued, and Kodes wound up pushing him. Twice. That's a big no-no, pushing a tournament referee. Gianfranco Cameli, the tournament director, immediately called the match for Zugarelli. According to news reports from the time, as Kodes walked off the court, he shouted, "Thieves!" at the tournament director and then, upon reaching the locker room, burst into tears. Meanwhile, the partisan Italian crowd, stirred by the on-court violence and then incensed by the premature end to what had been a fantastic match, was ready to burn the whole place down, despite the fact that their guy had won.

Back to my match with Zugarelli. I serve a bomb. The service linesman calls it out. I walk two steps forward, looking at the mark. I turn, and my eyes meet the umpire's.

A miracle happens. Truly a miracle. The umpire gets down off his chair, runs out, and checks the mark. He then puts both hands down to indicate the serve was in. Looks at Zugarelli and then runs back to his chair. The crowd is screaming bloody murder. The umpire says into his microphone, "I overrule the call; the ball was good. Zugarelli leads five points to four." Zuggy goes crazy, and the fans… well, it's bad.

Zugarelli's pointing to an out mark. The crowd is backing him one hundred percent. He walks over to talk to the umpire. He calls over the Italian service linesman. Arms start flying. Out comes Brunetti, the tournament referee. It's a zoo. I decide to sit down on my changeover chair and get some water while this scene plays out. Just as I am seated, something slams into the back of my chair. I turn around and see a whole orange peel lying on the court.

Fifteen minutes later, we resume the match. The overrule by the umpire still stands. It's 5-4, Zugarelli. The very next point turns into something special. This one point represents red clay court tennis at its best: some great defense and solid stroking of the ball. We're both hitting out. I'm juicing it. Every ball. Zuggy gets me on the run and hits a big, flat forehand down the line, off maybe the back of the tape. Very close. Very.

The baseline linesman signals out with his arm. The umpire doesn't get out of his chair. Zugarelli goes berserk. The crowd is right there with him. We're an inch from a riot. I retreat to the back of the court. I'm out of sight of the fans behind me, and I can see if anything is coming toward me.

Zuggy is now on my side of the court. Pointing at a mark. Pleading with the baseline linesman to get up and check it. He won't budge. It's total chaos. Even Dibbs and Solomon are yelling at me now. "Come on, Foro Vitzy! Hey, Foro Vitzy! Hey, Foro Vitzy!" And they're cracking up. It's bad. Zuggy is feeling screwed over by his own countrymen. It's the biggest match of his career. He had started to play really well. And now this.

Out comes Brunetti again. It's a madhouse. Another fifteen minutes, for sure. I stay against the backdrop on my side of the court this time. No telling what might get thrown at me if I go over to my chair now. I probably got off light with the orange peel.

They finally decide the ball is out. The call stands. It's five-all in the tie-breaker.

When Antonio "Zuggy" Zugarelli was a kid he had half of his right thumb cut off. That's the same hand he hits all his shots with. It's hard enough playing tennis with a whole thumb. But it's not the thumb that gets Zuggy in the end of our match. It's his head. His head is totally blown. I'm into the quarterfinals, 7-5 in the tiebreaker.

"I am glad I won because my hotel bill was about to break me," I'm quoted as saying in an Associated Press article published in newspapers worldwide the next day. Classic stuff. And it's the truth.

In the quarterfinals, Guillermo Vilas, who'd been stampeding through the tournament like a Brahman bull through a Buenos Aires sunflower field, finishes off the job my hotel bill had started. In the semifinals, however, he runs smack into a seventeen-year-old Swedish brick wall named Björn Borg. They play a marathon five-setter over two days (back then, the semifinals and final of the tournament were best of five sets), with Borg coming back from two sets down to take the match, 7-5, in the fifth. Later that same day he beats defending champion Ilie Nastase in the finals in straight sets for his first top-level singles title. A month later, Borg would win the French Open, the first of six titles he'd eventually claim at Roland Garros. And me? I picked up two thousand U.S. dollars for making it to that Italian Open quarterfinal. I got it in hundreds and fifties. I'd never seen that much cash in my life. Man, I was rich. More importantly, I had survived Foro Italico. I had survived the Colosseum. I had survived to fight another day on the pro tour.

Chapter 8

Haven't You Heard the News?

In the summer of 1977, I became the first professional athlete in any sport to compete in the Maccabiah Games. The Maccabiah Games are like the Jewish Olympics. They take place in Israel after the Summer Olympics. In the 1977 Maccabiah Games, 2,700 athletes from 33 counties participated in 26 different sports. I was automatically named to the USA Maccabiah team in '77 because I was the highest-ranked Jewish-American on the tour willing to miss three weeks of pro tournaments. At that time, I was number 77 in the world. My dad encouraged me to go. "You never know where this could lead," he said.

I was the top seed in the men's singles. I ended up winning the gold medal, defeating Larry Nagler in the final. Larry had been a star at UCLA a decade before my time there, sweeping the NCAA singles and doubles titles as a sophomore in 1960 and leading the team to the national title that year and the next. He also played for two years on the

UCLA basketball team under Coach John Wooden. Larry was a transplanted New Yorker, still living in Los Angeles at the time of our match. Heck of an athlete and a really nice guy.

After the match, on Center court at the Ramat Hasharon Tennis Center, with the gold medal around my neck, and photographers snapping shots, Joseph "Josi" Stabholz comes up to me and introduces himself. Today, Joseph Stabholz has a successful law practice in Tel Aviv. Back then, he was the nonplaying Israeli Davis Cup captain.

Josi asked me if I would like "to make aliyah" and play Davis Cup for Israel. I didn't even know what aliyah was, or if I wanted to play Davis Cup for Israel. I mean, I'm twenty-six years old and in a foreign country. And I'm an American, right? I thanked Josi and told him I'd think about it.

Later I learned that aliyah was Hebrew for immigration to Israel. I also learned that, under the Jewish Law of Return, I could apply for Israeli citizenship and immigrate to the Holy Land, and after only ninety days in the country, the State of Israel would award me citizenship. That way I could play for the Israeli Davis Cup team and keep my U.S. citizenship.

Still, I wasn't sure. But on the flight back to New York with the USA Maccabiah team — gold medal still around my neck — I started thinking back to Cossacks and Germans.

I never knew my great-grandfather on my dad's side. But in 1975 I wore a beard. A thick one. My father showed me pictures of my great-grandfather (his grandfather). He also had a beard. What a striking resemblance. Not only in facial features but also in our physical build.

In the late 19th century, my great-grandfather on my dad's side was a farmer with a prosperous turpentine business in Ukraine. One day in Russia, the natives got restless. The Czar said to some of his guys, "Okay go ahead and have some fun." Cossacks don't like turpentine farms, especially those run by Jews. And so the barn was burned down. But the Jews in Ukraine stuck together. They helped my great-grandfather rebuild, and for two and a half years, everything returned to normal.

You can probably guess what happened next. The natives got restless again. Down came that rebuilt barn, and my great-grandfather's daughter (my grandmother) got roughed up, too. Not a pretty sight. Cossacks didn't like Jews, and Jews didn't like Cossacks. A few weeks later, my great-grandfather took his family and sailed for the New York Harbor.

That brings me to the Germans. In the early 20th century, my grandfather on my mom's side, Kazimierz Luszczak, was a carefree eighteen-year-old living in Krakow, a city which at that time was in the Russian-controlled area of Poland. Then

World War I began, and everything came crashing down.

Every male between the ages of seventeen and thirty-five was conscripted into the Russian military. Russia was at war with Germany and Austria-Hungary, both of which also controlled land in what had formerly been part of the sovereign nation of Poland. One week later, five hundred men carrying muskets were marching south from Krakow on their way to get mowed down by modern rapid-fire machine guns manned by the Germans. Pop — that's what we called my grandfather — was one of them.

Years later Pop recalled, "Every man knew we were marching to be slaughtered. We had no chance against the German infantry. It was a hot summer day, even for Poland. Scorching heat. We were marching in rows of two. Five hundred men in columns of two, each along the road. There was a feeling of doom. It was horrible. Just then, a convoy of trucks came upon us. Polish trucks heading south with reinforcements. We all stepped to the side of the road. The dust was thick. The convoy of trucks was long. Finally, the reinforcement brigade passed, the dust finally rose, and the soldiers stepped back onto the road continuing their death march south."

All except Kazimierz "Pop" Luszczak. He had a good twenty-minute head start into the woods and never looked back. He ran and ran and didn't stop running until he was safely back at home. The law decreed that any deserters would be shot. Under the cover of darkness, Pop's father transported him to a cousin's house outside Krakow, two hours away. From there, his cousin smuggled him to a port, and Kazimierz Luszczak sailed to America. He wound up in New Haven, Connecticut as Charles Lustick. Not speaking a single word of English. All alone. But alive.

Fast-forward three decades. The Nazis moved into Poland. Established ghettos. All Jews were rounded up and put in work camps or ghettos. The concentration camp in Krakow was called Plaszow. When the Nazis put their Final Solution to the Jewish Question into action, my grandfather's entire family — mother, father, sisters, brother, aunts, uncles, and cousins — got shipped to Auschwitz. Twenty-two members of the Krakow family never returned home.

On that plane ride to New York after the Maccabiah Games, all these thoughts were going through my head. So by the time President Feigel of the Israel Tennis Association (ITA) called me, I had made my decision. I was ready to make aliyah and kick some ass.

***

"Steve, you need a ride back to the hotel?" Josi, the captain of the Israeli Davis Cup Team, asks me.

"Sure Josi. Toda Raba," I say — which is Hebrew for "Thank you very much" or "Thanks a lot." In addition to those few words and Boker Tov — which is Hebrew for "Good morning" — that is about it for me when it comes to the language.

It's March 11th, 1978. I'm at the Ramat Hasharon Tennis Center outside Tel Aviv. Israel vs. Austria is seven days away. Davis Cup. Regulation. Second division. First-round tie. Davis Cup matches (also known as "ties") are played over three days from Friday to Sunday. The first team with three out of the five matches wins. The winner advances with a shot to move up to the top group of sixteen countries. Israel has a real chance. I'm playing number one singles and doubles, too.

"Hey, Josi, can you give Paul a ride, too?" I ask. "He wants to go back to the hotel."

"Of course, Steve," Josi says. "No problem."

Paul "Henski" Cohen had traveled with me to Israel to serve as the "Honorary" team coach. I first met Paul at the UCLA Sunset tennis courts in Los Angeles back when I was in school. Paul was a stockbroker who had an unusual obsession with tennis. After the market would close, he would come out and hang around the Sunset courts. He befriended all the guys on the UCLA team. Coach Bassett thought it was all pretty harmless, and it was. Paul lived four blocks from the UCLA campus with his wife, Jane, and their two little kids. The guys on the team would hang out at Paul's house. Jane would cook up some great dinners, and Paul had the best weed in Southern California. This was the '70s, remember, early '70s.

After graduating, I kept in touch with Paul and Jane. I had a place on the beach, and when I was in town I'd stop over and have dinner at their house. Some of the current UCLA tennis guys would be there, so I would get updated on the team's progress and results. It was during one of those visits that I told Paul I was heading to Israel to play in the Davis Cup. Paul had quit the market and was now teaching tennis full time in the Los Angeles area. He went on to coach my buddy Harold Solomon on the pro tour and later John McEnroe. Paul begged me to take him to Israel for the Austria "tie." Now he's sitting in the back seat of Josi's car as we pull up to the Tel Aviv Hilton.

"Tel Aviv is safe. Very safe," Josi says looking at us. "It's safer than the States."

I couldn't have agreed more. It seemed like every third person was a soldier. Male and female, in uniform. And every one of them was carrying what looked to me like a sawed-off machine gun on their shoulder. I later found out that half-machine gun is called an Uzi.

"What time are we practicing this afternoon?" I call out to Paul, as I head to my room.

I know our usual routine by heart. Morning session: Practice from 10:00 a.m. to noon. Back to the hotel for lunch. Nap. Paul would come to my room at 2:00 p.m., and by 2:15 p.m. we would be in the rental car, heading back to the tennis center. Afternoon session: Practice from 3:00 p.m. to 5:00 p.m. And then physical training session with Melleck, our Davis Cup fitness trainer from 5:00 p.m. to 6:00 p.m. But there is a barbecue at the Tel Aviv Country Club at 4:30 p.m. that Paul and I had been invited to.

Paul wants to go to the tennis center and hit, then go to the barbecue. I didn't want to go the barbecue. Not as enthusiastic about the hit. I'm feeling pretty beat.

I'm in a deep, deep slumber. Almost don't hear the knocking on the door. I slowly get up and look at the hotel clock by my bed. Two o'clock. I go to the door. My body is demanding more rest.

"Hey, Henski, come back at four o'clock and we'll head over to the barbecue. I'm not practicing anymore today. I need the rest."

"Okay, I'll come back then," Paul says. He does, and we start getting ready to leave the hotel for the country club. But

I'm still feeling wiped. No sense in pushing it. There'll be plenty of other barbecues. This is Davis Cup. I make the call and decide the barbecue is out. Got to rest up.

Around 4:10 p.m., I'm resting in my room when I hear a knock at the door. I open it. It's Paul, and he looks ashen. "What's the matter?" I ask.

"Haven't you heard the news?" he says. "There has been a terrorist attack in Tel Aviv. It's all over the news."

"What happened?" I ask.

"It's not totally clear, but we can't leave the hotel. We're on lockdown," he says.

Paul and I watch the news for the rest of the day and night. Facts start to come in. Not all the details are immediately clear. But the full story that eventually comes out is horrific.

At 1:45 p.m. that same day, while I was napping in my room at the Tel Aviv Hilton, two rubber boats carrying eleven armed militants from the Palestinian Liberation Organization faction, Al Fatah, had landed ashore near a seaside kibbutz called Ma'agan Michael, about forty miles north of Tel Aviv. They'd set out completing a two-day journey from southern Lebanon.

Taking pictures on the beach that day was thirty-nine-year-old American photographer Gail Rubin. The militants approached her, asking where they were. Then these supposed "freedom fighters" murdered this unarmed civilian and made their way up to the main road, the Tel Aviv-Haifa highway (also known as Coastal Highway). There they stopped a taxi, killing its passengers while the driver managed to escape. Soon, they captured a tourist bus. By this time the police have been alerted. A roadblock is set up outside the Tel Aviv Country Club. The bus is stopped and there is a fifteen-minute firefight.

Tel Aviv is on lockdown. The Israel Defense Forces (IDF) had to make sure there weren't any more terrorists from the Palestinian Liberation Organization (PLO) on the loose. So much for Tel Aviv being safer than the States.

Here's the timeline:

The PLO members had been on Haifa Road between 2:15 p.m. and 2:25 p.m. If Paul and I had stuck to our usual schedule that day, we would have been on that road by 2:15 p.m., heading to practice. The thought was scary. Sleeping was difficult.

The next morning, we learn that IDF could not confirm whether all the Palestinian terrorists were killed and were still searching the area.

The hotel receptionist tells Paul, in pretty good English, that the lockdown has only been lifted in certain areas of Tel Aviv. The tennis center has already been searched once, but the road to the center is closed. What he fails to mention for some reason — maybe because he doesn't know — is that there is a twenty-four hour curfew in place in the area around the country club.

The next thing I know, Paul is over at the Tel Aviv car rental booth asking for directions.

"Hey, what's going on?" I ask.

"We're leaving now," Paul says. "The road is closed."

Off we go to the Ramat Hasharon Tennis Center. Normally, it's about a fifteen-minute drive. Today it takes forty-five minutes. Around and around we go. Paul won't quit. We finally make it. Paul drives right up to the front entrance. The gates are locked. There's nobody around. Nobody. It's empty.

"We'll climb the fence," Paul says.

"Paul, are you serious?" I ask.

"Come on," he says, and gets out of the car. He opens up the trunk, grabs our racket bags and the bag of balls, and starts walking toward the fence.

"Hey, Paul, wait a minute," I say, getting out of the car. He throws my racket bag over the fence and says, "You first." Then he throws his racquet bag and the bag of balls over, too.

I start climbing the fence. This is crazy. I get to the top, and just as I'm putting one leg over to the other side, out of the corner of my eye, I see some movement in the orange grove, right next to the tennis courts. My heart stops. I freeze. I have never been this scared in my life. It's so quiet. The wind is blowing, and it's very, very eerie. A guy comes out. A solider. Then another. All of a sudden a chopper comes out of nowhere and starts circling us. I can see six guys hanging out, looking down at us with rifles. *This is the end*, I think.

But then I notice the soldiers have Uzis. They start yelling in Hebrew. It's IDF, patrolling the area. Paul runs over to them. He starts telling them about how we have the Davis Cup in two days and want to practice. They say go ahead.

We play two hours. Then I do one hour of the Melleck Fitness program. Minus Melleck. I guess he couldn't make it.

The Austrians come in cocky. Hans Kary, their number one player, with whom I'd actually played doubles several times on the tour, hasn't brushed up on his Holocaust history apparently. Kary tells me he's going to make a lampshade out of me. But we're on Jewish soil, not European. I take Kary, 6-2 in the fifth set. What a sweet win. Very sweet.

The next day is doubles. Shlomo Glickstein and I go down in three straight sets to Kary and Austria's number two, Peter Feigl.

It's the third day and Austria is leading two matches to one. I play Feigl and take him down in straight sets, 7-5, 6-2, 6-2, to tie it up at two-all. Unfortunately, we lose the "tie," three matches to two. Even though we don't advance, I know, my great-grandfather would have been proud of me.

Steve (right) at Holabird Sports with James Blake (left), former world No. 4 professional tennis player.

Steve (middle) with Ron "Magic" Shelton (left) and Rasmus Keinicke (right) at the Krulevitz summer tennis camp.

Steve (left) with Harold Solomon (right), former World No. 5 and U.S. Davis Cup player.

Steve (right) shaking hands with Andre Agassi (left), former World No. 1 professional tennis player, at the 2008 Washington Tennis & Education Foundation VIP Round Robin.

Steve (right) at the 1977 Maccabiah Games where he won the gold metal after beating Larry Nagler (left) at the Ramat Hasharon Tennis Center in Tel Aviv, Israel.

Steve (left) coaching Jaime Yzaga (right), former World No. 18 professional tennis player.

Pam Shriver with Steve's
daughter, Stephannie,
after winning the 2000
Maryland State
Sportsmanship award.

Steve serving at the
Prudential-Bache
Grand Championships
35 and Over Circuit
Tour.

Steve (right) with Stan
Smith (left) U.S. Open
and Wimbledon
Champion and former
No. 1 player in the world.

UCLA Men's Varsity
Tennis Team in 1973.

Steve with wife, Ann
"Minky" Krulevitz

The Krulevitz
Clan.

Counselors and true
Vikings from the
Krulevitz summer
tennis camp.

Steve (right) with Ilie
Nastase (left), U.S. Open
and French Open
Champion and former
World No. 1 professional
tennis player.

Steve (right) with Eddie
"Fast" Dibbs (left),
former World No. 5 and
one of the true characters
in the sport of tennis.

Steve (right) with
Chilean professional
tennis player, Patricio
"Pato" Cornejo (left)
in Indianapolis.

Chapter 9

My One Shot

It's the third week of July 1978 in Washington, D.C., and it's hot. Deathly hot. I'm sitting at the top of the bleachers of the William H.G. FitzGerald Tennis Stadium at 16th and Kennedy Streets NW. The Washington Star International Tennis Championships is one of the Grand Prix stops on the summer tour. From 1970 to 1989 the Grand Prix tennis circuit was the men's professional tennis tour.

It's Tuesday, late afternoon, and I'm relaxing with my buddies Eddie "Fast" Dibbs and Uri Emsellem.

This tournament is one of the biggest events in D.C. during the summer. I have played it with minimal success almost every year since 1970, the summer after my first year of college, when I went up against the top seed, Ilie Nastase, in the first round. He took me out, 6-2, 7-5. Pretty heavy stuff for a nineteen-year-old kid.

The next time I play the tournament, two years later, I am

up against Rod Laver in the first round. That's what they call the luck of the *draw*. Laver was a couple weeks shy of thirty-four years old. He beat me, 6-4, 6-2.

Afterwards, I happened to be on my way out of the locker room just as Laver was heading in. "Rocket, any tips you can give me on my game?" I ask him. Laver glanced over his shoulder at me and then said, "Just keep playing."

I flashed back to Don Budge. Also to Pancho Gonzales, whom I'd asked one day in L.A. to help me with my serve. "Just hit it harder," Pancho said to me. Sure, John McEnroe, Björn Borg, Pete Sampras, Andre Agassi, Roger Federer, and Rafael Nadal are legends, the greatest players ever. But when I was a kid, these players were not even born yet. Taking lessons from Maury Schwartzman down at Druid Hill Park, I only heard about three players — Don Budge, Pancho Gonzales, and Rod Laver. Why? Because when the pro circuit stopped in Baltimore, Maury was in the first row watching, memorizing, and imagining. That is how Maury became such a great tennis instructor. He watched, analyzed, and then incorporated the techniques of these players into his own teaching methods. I would try and hit my backhand like Budge, serve like Gonzales, stay cool and calm on the court like Laver. These three tennis players were not mortals; they were gods in Maury's eyes and they soon became gods in my eyes. Every lesson for five years that is all I knew — Budge, Gonzales, and Laver. I wanted to be like them. I wanted to play like them.

Don Budge, Pancho Gonzales, and Rod Laver will always be tennis gods. But when I asked them for a little advice, a little help, they were not interested in me. That is not to say that they did not help a lot of other kids (maybe they did). That would be unfair, but I can only go by my own experience. There was a lesson here — if anyone asks for advice on their tennis game or tennis career, take a second and give it. Be a Maury Schwartzman or a Glenn Bassett.

***

Now I'm twenty-seven. Single. Traveling every week. Making a little coin and living, basically, a dream. One day at a time. Loving life. But I've got no love in my life.

Ninety-nine-point-nine percent of the time, if you meet a female at a tournament, nothing much happens. What you try to do instead is set it up for down the road. Time is your enemy. The tour stays in a city for just one week, unless it's one of the Slams, which runs for two weeks. That's why, right this second, I have to think fast. This could be my one shot.

"Hello. Hello. Excuse me?" I call out to the dark-haired girl below.

The day before, sitting under the players' tent was a real beauty. Maybe it was the long black hair. Or maybe it was that she was hardly wearing any clothes. Couldn't blame her for that. Brutal, brutal heat. She stayed for a while at the John Fitzgerald Tennis Center, and then disappeared into the volunteers' tent. Exceptional. Now there she is again.

Come on, Vitz, think. Think faster. Tomorrow is Wednesday. The week is just about over. "Excuse me," I say again to the dark-haired girl. She stops and looks up. Think fast. "Would you mind bringing us some Cokes?" I'm hoping she really is a volunteer and that she'll fall for this ploy.

"How many Cokes do you want?" she asks. I turn quickly to Eddie and Uri, and ask, "Coke? Coke?"

"Yeah, yeah," they say. I turn and look back down at the girl. "Three please," I say. "Thank you."

A few minutes later, she appears up in the bleachers with three Cokes. She looks even better today. Long legs. Broad shoulders. Tan. Long black hair. And the shortest shorts and lowest-cut tank top imaginable.

"What's your name?" I ask her. She looks at me. The look feels familiar.

"Ann," she says.

"Hey, thanks for the drinks," I say. "It's a little chilly up here." I'm trying to be funny.

"This is my friend Eddie," I say, pointing to Dibbs. "He's the number three seed in the tournament behind Connors and Gottfried. And this is my good friend Uri. He has a hair salon in Georgetown. Best salon in D.C. He cuts all the players' hair. Except mine. He loses too many scissors on me." I'm trying to be funny again.

"You working for the tournament?" Eddie asks.

"I'm a volunteer driver for the week," she says.

"That figures," Eddie says, turning to Uri, "the only week the entire year I rent a car. We all laugh.

Ann turns to me and asks, "What's your name?"

"That's Vitz!" Eddie says.

"I'm Steve," I say, "and, really, thanks for the Cokes. You saved us up here."

"That's okay," she says. "It'll put lead in your pencil." Uri and I look at each other. Did we hear that right?

"You from around here?" Eddie asks.

"Alexandria," Ann says.

"Why are you driving people around?" Eddie asks.

"Some friends asked me to join them. I just finished

school at the University of Virginia and was free this week," Ann says.

I perk up at that. Don't feel the heat or humidity now. UVA, hey, that's a great school. This girl not only has looks but is obviously smart. Uri is clearly soaking all of this in, too.

Then out of the blue, Eddie says, "Hey, Vitz, why don't you ask Ann out? Come on, ask her out."

This was embarrassing. I didn't know what to say other than, "It's probably not a good time right now."

Eddie was loving this. It's possible he was feeling more full of himself than usual that day. Eddie was in the midst of the best year of his professional career. Just the day before, the new rankings came out, and Eddie had moved up from number six to number five in the world, a position he'd maintain until the very last day of the year, the highest ranking of his career. He was also on his way to winning the most prize money of any player on the tour that year. Just shy of $600,000. More than Connors. More than Borg. More than all of us. He'd wind up losing in the final of this D.C. tournament to Connors, 7-5, 7-5.

"Come on, Vitz," Eddie says again. "Ask her out."

"Ed, forget it," I say.

Ann looks slightly bemused by this fraternity house act.

"I have to get back to the tent," she says. "They're probably wondering where I am."

We say our goodbyes, and she splits.

"I gotta get back to the shop," Uri says, and he takes off, too.

"What time do you play tonight?" I ask Eddie, the big-mouth.

"Second match on Stadium court," Eddie says. "So I'm going to head back to the hotel now."

I stop by the players' tent and grab a water. I decide to head over to the volunteer tent. People are milling around. I spot Ann sitting at a desk by a fan. Suddenly, those lyrics from the Bob Dylan song "Like a Rolling Stone" start playing in my head: "When you got nothing, you got nothing to lose."

I approach her. She looks up. "Hi again," she says. "Do you need transportation?"

"I have a car," I say. "I drove over from Baltimore. That's where I'm from."

She looks at me like, "What gives?" So I just blurt out, "So, how about it?"

She looks at me like I'm nuts and says, "How about what?" I feel foolish. I lower my head sheepishly and say,

"How about going out with me?"

"Are you asking me out?" she asks. I'm figuring this isn't working out. But I say, "Yes. Would you like to go out with me?" I'm thinking, at this juncture, no chance. I figure she's going to say, any second now, "Sorry, I can't, I have a boyfriend." But, instead, she says, "When?" I'm shocked. "How about Thursday night?" I ask. "Okay," she says.

Just then I remember that Thursday night is Susie Trees' annual tournament party at her house in Georgetown. Can't miss that, right? So I say to Ann, "Would Friday be good? I just remembered I have something Thursday night."

"Friday is good," she says. I'm really into this now. "Let's get some dinner Friday night," I say. "Okay," she says. Perfect! Can't wait until Friday. Meanwhile, let's stay focused on tennis. After all, this is supposed to be my profession, right?

The next day, Wednesday, rolls around, and I'm out of the singles competition. Still alive in the doubles though. Which is great. Maybe Ann will come to a match.

For this tournament, as for all tournaments, I have followed the most important rule in doubles, which is get the best partner you possibly can. For this big summer pro tournament, I have done just that. Bruce Manson. Bruce is out of Los Angeles. He went to the University of Southern California (USC). A rivalry school. No worries. Those days are long over. This isn't college tennis. This is for real. Bruce is a lefty. Even better. That makes for an attractive doubles partner. Plus, he's good. Bruce is about five years younger than I am. In 1980 and 1981, he'd go on to team up with my old UCLA teammate Brian Teacher for five titles.

In our third-round match, we're up against the fourth seed, Victor Pecci from Paraguay, who reached a career-high singles ranking of number nine in the world, and Wojtek Fibak from Poland, who reached a career-high singles ranking of number 10 in the world. Tough team. Especially on the dirt.

We're scheduled to be the fourth match on court one after the 11:00 a.m. starting time. So Bruce and I figure we'll get on court around 5:00 p.m. This is good because the after-work crowd will start to filter in. It should be a great atmosphere.

Bruce and I practice around noon. Solid workout. Afterwards, we head out to get some lunch together. Good bonding. Stick together. We finish lunch and still have some time before the match. You know the pro tour: hurry up and wait. Bruce needs his space so he goes off by himself after lunch. Everyone has their own way of preparing for a match. That's cool. So I go and see if Ann is around. And she is.

"Hey, how are you?" I say. "I'm playing doubles at five

o'clock over on court one if you're around. The guys we play are tough. But if we win, we're in the quarterfinals." I'm firm about asking her to come. I really want her to watch us play. Well, me play. It's a strategic move, to be honest. You know. Ann comes out. I'm pumped. If Bruce and I win, it's a rush. If we lose, at least Ann has seen a little part of my life, so to speak. It's a win-win. And doubles is fun to watch.

Guess what? Ann shows up at the match in the second set. She sits right on the bleachers. Bruce and I win. We beat Pecci and Fibak, 6-4, 6-2. It is a good pro doubles clay court match. Ann stays until the end. I'm excited she came.

Bruce and I play again Friday. We could be playing Arthur Ashe and Bob Hewitt, the seventh seed, if they win tomorrow. This is great. We have the chance to play some really great players. And I have a date for dinner Friday night. It's a good week so far.

Susie Trees' party is pretty good. She caters it, and a lot of people show up. But, for some reason, I'm not into it. Not at all. I'm already thinking about the next day. The potential Ashe-Hewitt doubles match and a date with Ann. I'm pumped.

The next morning I call over to the tournament desk and find out that the schedule is out. Ashe-Hewitt won late last night. Bruce and I play sometime after 3:00 p.m. on court one.

I call Bruce, and we agree to warm up at noon. Stick to the same routine since it's working. We practice and have lunch together. Stay calm. Stay relaxed. Stay focused.

I see Ann and start telling her about the match. "This is big. We play sometime after 3:00 p.m. on court one," I say. Then I ask her, not in a demanding way, "Did you bring some clothes for dinner?"

In a very nonchalant and uninterested way, she says, "Well I forgot my clothes." That's not a good sign.

"Well, we can still grab some dinner after the match," I say, undaunted. "There's this Japanese steak house in Bethesda. It's casual dress."

"Have you ever been there?" I ask her. She doesn't say anything. Lights on, nobody is home. Nothing. No emotion.

"It'll be fun," I say. "You sit on the floor, and they cook the food right in front of you." Still nothing. Not a word. Wow!

"Okay, well, I'll see you later," I say. *That was a bit weird*, I think.

Bruce and I play some really solid doubles against Ashe and Hewitt. We lose 7-6 in the third. Ann stops by for about four games and then takes off. She disappears. I'm still feeling good, however. Hey, you can't win 'em all. Bruce and I played well. Ashe and Hewitt were hot. They ended up winning the tournament. We were the only opponents to even take a set off them, and that included the young, fifth seeded team of Peter Fleming and John McEnroe, whom they knocked off in the semis, and the top seed of Raul Ramirez and my boyhood friend Fred McNair, whom they beat for the title.

Yep, Bruce and I had a nice tournament. We agree to play some more doubles together. I like playing with the guy. He's a shot maker. Get the best doubles player you can find. I go off to get my prize money. The tournament is over for me.

At the tournament tent, I have transportation call and get me a reservation out of Baltimore for a Saturday early-evening flight to Louisville. That's the next stop on the summer tour. That works well for me. I'll stay in D.C. for the night. Drive back home to Baltimore in the morning and head to Louisville tomorrow evening. I play singles first round on Monday.

It's after six. The three sets of doubles we played took almost two hours. "Have you seen Ann?" I ask a girl at the transportation desk.

"She left," the girl says. "I think she went home." Wow. That sucks. I don't have her phone number. I don't even know her last name. That is not good. I start to head for the locker room to get my gear, and I remember that one of my best

112

friends from high school who is an attorney is working as a sports agent for ProServ (also known as Professional Service Inc.).

ProServ was created in 1970 in Washington, D.C. by former professional tennis player and United States Davis Cup captain Donald Dell and his friend Frank Craighill. Their first clients were Donald's Davis Cup teammates, Arthur Ashe and Stan Smith. Initially focused on tennis, the company would grow to become among the world's largest sports marketing, athlete management, even production, and TV companies.

I walk over to the players' tent and ask the girl there if she has ProServ's office number. She dials it and puts the phone to her ear. "It's transferring me to a directory," she says.

"Does the name Rick Schaeffer come up?" I ask her. A few moments later she presses a key on the phone and then hands it to me. It rings a few times, and then Rick picks up. He's still in the office.

"Hey, Doc. It's Dave," I say. "What's up?"

"Doc" and "Dave" nicknames are from high school when we watched the TV series "The Fugitive," starring David Janssen as Dr. Richard Kimble. Dr. Kimble is convicted of killing his wife. On the way to be executed, he escapes and begins searching for the one-armed man he saw fleeing from his house the night his wife was killed. It was our favorite.

"Where are you, Dave?" Doc asks.

"I'm calling from the tournament desk," I say.

"How'd the doubles go? I saw you played Ashe and Hewitt. Sorry I couldn't make it out this week. It has been really busy," Doc says.

"We lost in the third," I say. "What are you doing for dinner tonight though? You want to grab a bite?"

"That would be great," Doc says. "Let me finish up here. I'll see you in about thirty minutes.

"That sounds good, Doc," I say." I'll leave you a ticket at will call under your name. I'll be in the players' tent."

I head over to will call and leave Rick his ticket. I start walking back to the tent, and spot Ann coming up the walkway with a group of friends.

"Hey," I say, "How are you? We lost 7-6 in the third set. Do you still want to go for dinner? I wasn't sure where you were so I invited an old high school friend who is working here in D.C."

She looks at me and says, "I'm not sure. I didn't bring anything to wear." And walks away with her friends. Oh well, what can you do?

Rick "Doc" Schaeffer shows up. We graduated from the Park School together in 1969. He went off to Case Western Reserve in Ohio for undergrad, then the University of Maryland for law school. Now he is working at ProServ.

"Are you ready for some dinner?" I ask.

"Sure, Dave," Doc says, "but I heard Eddie is playing doubles tonight with Ralston." That's Dennis Ralston. He was ranked number one in the late '60s, early '70s. Ralston was out of Bakersfield, California. He had been a star at USC. The press labeled him "Dennis the Menace." He had a temper on the court. I knew him a little from some tournaments, but he wasn't anything like the press made him out to be. We got along fine. I really liked him.

"Can we watch a couple games of the doubles?" Doc asks. "I haven't seen any tennis the whole week."

Rick played number three singles on our high school tennis team. He is a big tennis and football fan.

"That's fine," I say.

We head over to Center court to watch Eddie and Ralston in their third-round match against another pair of Americans: Billy Martin and Bill Scanlon. We sit in the players' section, right behind the court. During the next changeover, Ann and her friends come and sit down, twenty or so chairs to our left.

"Hey, Doc, do you see that girl on the end over there?" I say. "I asked her to dinner tonight, but she blew me off."

"Plenty of fish in the sea," he says. Sure thing. But I kind of liked that fish.

Rick is really enjoying the doubles. It's a fun match to watch. Ralston has great, great technique on his volleys, and Eddie is being Eddie, playing to the crowd, having fun.

During the match, I turn around and see a guy I know sitting five rows back and two sections over — Nick Gordan (which is not his real name). Nick is a friend of Eddie's. I met him a few times down in Miami Beach with Eddie. Nick ran the numbers racket for Meyer Lansky in South Florida. Lansky was one of the biggest mobsters of all time.

"Hey, Rick, I see an old friend," I say. "I'll be right back." Have to pay my respects, of course. I head over to Nick during the next changeover. He gives me a big hug, and we joke around about the time he passed out in his soup at Embers down on the beach. Everyone thought he'd had a heart attack, and they started rifling through his clothes, pulling out betting tickets from wherever you can gamble — racetrack, dog track, college football — guns, and cash.

After a few minutes he wakes up with all these guys'

hands all over him and screams out, "what the hell is going on here?" Everyone stops and then starts laughing. We laugh. I make some small talk.

"How are things on the beach?" I ask him.

"Everything is cool," Nick says. "How are you doing, Steve?"

"Great. But it would be going even better if that girl over there would come with me and my friend for dinner," I say, pointing in the direction of the dark-haired girl.

"Which girl?" Nick asks as he looks over to where I'm pointing. Now, I wish I never said anything. I really do.

"Which one?" Nick asks.

"Nah, don't worry about it," I say.

"Which one?" he asks again, still looking.

"Forget it," I say, "just enjoy the tennis."

Nick looks at me. "Fine," I say, "second girl in from the very end with the dark hair."

"Don't move a muscle," Nick says, and he takes off toward Ann and her friends. The guy's in his sixties, but he still moves like a cat. Wish I hadn't said anything.

Nick muscles his way right in next to Ann and stays there

until the next changeover. Then he rushes back over to me and takes his seat.

"Ask her again," Nick says.

"I should ask her again?" I ask.

"Go ahead," Nick says.

"Okay, man," I say.

"Go ahead, ask her again," Nick says.

I return to my seat next to Doc. "Hey, I'm going to ask the dark-haired girl out again for dinner, but we have to go eat on the next changeover," I say to Doc.

"Okay, Dave," Doc says.

I walk up to Ann, and say, "This is my friend Rick. We're going for dinner. Can you come along?"

"I have some jeans in the car!" she says. "Would that be okay to wear?"

"Perfect," I say, and she gets up and walks out of the stadium with us. Sometimes it pays to have friends.

The Japanese Steak House is just like I remember it: awesome. You take off your shoes. You sit on the floor around a table. The cook cooks the food right there. It's one of my favorite places. And it's close to the courts.

Our waitress comes over and says, "Sake?" What is Sake? I quietly ask Rick what it is, and he says, "Japanese rice wine." I had never heard of it. But I've got a date to impress. So I tell the waitress to bring it out.

The waitress comes back a few minutes later with some ice waters and a pot of Sake, I guess, and three cups. The Sake is warm, and strong. It's too strong for me. Rick takes a sip, and I can see he's struggling a bit. I drink a few sips, and it immediately goes to my head. Ann, meanwhile, takes down the entire first cup, no problem. She asks for a refill. Wow. I'm impressed.

We have a great meal. I stick to water, and Rick gets a couple of Cokes. Ann drinks the entire rest of the pot of Sake by herself. My kind of woman.

It's now 10:15 p.m., getting kind of late. It has been a long day. I don't have that much time. Got to ditch Doc. Two is company, three is a crowd. Doc wants to order some ice cream. Bad idea.

"Where do you live?" I ask Doc.

"On Canal Street," he says, "not far from Georgetown."

"I'll drop you off," I say. "I have to head back to Baltimore tonight." Lie. "I have an early flight out to Louisville tomorrow morning." Double lie. Hey, if you're going to lie, make it a good one. "Can't do the ice cream," I say. "Maybe next time."

I wouldn't say I was Mario Andretti behind the wheel. But I'm fairly sure I made record time from Bethesda to Georgetown that night. Then Ann and I head back to Rock Creek Park.

"I have to stop by the house before we go back to your car," I say. "I'm staying with a family friend." Ann is easy going. Maybe it's the Sake. She says, "Okay."

I was staying in Chevy Chase, on Western Avenue, with my mom's best childhood friend Genie Blechman. My mom is a Washingtonian. Genie had a beautiful house in Chevy Chase, along with a husband and two grown kids who no longer lived at home. I had stayed at the Blechman's for a number of years while playing in this tournament. They had plenty of room and were generous, kind folks.

We get to Genie's house on Western Run. "I'm back, but I'm here with Ann Gorneva from the tournament," I yell up the stairs to Genie. "I have to run her back to the courts in a little."

"Okay, Stevie!" Genie yells back.

Ann and I go into the living room and sit on the couch. I turn on a lamp. We start talking, and pretty soon, we're kissing. Good, long kisses. Things are heating up.

Suddenly, Genie's daughter Peggy appears in the entranceway to the living room. She had taken the train down from New York for the weekend. I'm startled.

"Hi, Peggy," I say. "This is Ann." We compose ourselves, and Peggy walks away.

"I should be getting back to my car," Ann says. We leave and drive to the parking lot at 16th and Kennedy Streets N.W.

"You live in Alexandria?" I say.

"Yes," Ann says.

"Well, do you know the way?" I ask.

"I think so," she says, not sounding too confident.

"You go up 16th Street and turn left at the last light," I say. "That is Georgia Avenue which takes you to Interstate 495, toward Northern Virginia."

She doesn't look very attentive.

"Look, follow me," I say. "I'll take you to 495."

***

The Louisville tournament is unfortunately short and sweet for me. I was out of the singles draw by Monday afternoon, going down in straight sets to Ivan Molina from

Colombia. On Tuesday evening, Bruce and I win our first-round doubles match against Molina and Patricio Cornejo, of Chile. But Wednesday early afternoon, we are knocked out of the draw by the sixth seed, Mike Cahill and Terry Moor, another pair of Americans, 7-6 in the third. I'm out of the tournament.

Now I've got some time on my hands. It's never a good thing on the pro tour to have too much time. You can get into trouble when you have too much time. Indianapolis doesn't start until Monday. What should I do? Hanging around tournaments after you lose is a drag. It's pretty depressing. I could be back in Baltimore by tonight. Do some training at home for a few days. Start mentally fresh in Indiana. Maybe even call Ann and see if she wants to get together in Alexandria for dinner. It's not far from Baltimore. I have her number now, so I call.

The phone rings a few times and then Ann answers. "Hello," she says.

"Hey, what's going on?" I say.

"Not much," she says.

I get right to the point and ask, "Do you want to get dinner on Friday night?"

"Sure," Ann says.

"Great," I say. "I'll pick you up at seven. I'll call you tomorrow night and get your address and directions."

On Friday night at seven o'clock, I pull up to 5414 Forest Avenue in Alexandria, Virginia. It's the end of July 1978. I knock on the front door. Nobody answers. I knock again. Nothing. Wow, this is weird. I walk back out to the street and look at the mailbox. 5-4-1-4. Yep, I'm at the right place. I go back to the door and knock harder this time. Still no answer.

I walk back down the walkway toward my car. I notice that on the side of the house is another walkway that leads to what looks like the backyard. I follow it, open the gate slightly and call out, "Ann? Ann?"

I hear a voice that's definitely not Ann's cry out, "Over here, over here!" The voice has a foreign accent. I walk into the backyard, and to the left watering the bushes is a blonde woman. Topless. Whoa! The topless woman doesn't look at me. She doesn't even flinch. Just calls out, "Minky! Minky!"

"Go in the house. The door is there," she says and turns to show me. Full throttle. Totally exposed. No shame. No embarrassment. I'm a complete stranger.

I soon find out that this is Ann's mother, Sieglinde Penzkover Gorneva. They called her "Siegi" in Europe but "Linda" in the States. Blonde hair. Blue eyes. Full Aryan from

Munich, West Germany. She married Stanko Gornev from Provadia, Bulgaria. European roots. Stanko was studying law in Berlin when WWII started and couldn't make it back to Bulgaria. It was too dangerous. Borders were closing. He was laying low in Berlin and that's when he met Siegi. She was modeling at the time. A total bombshell. They hit it off immediately and decided to make their way down to the Bavarian Alps to Garmisch Partenkirchen, Germany where Siegi's grandmother lived. It was an out-of-the-way place. A ski resort. And Stanko was a foreigner. Good move. They hung out there during the war. Survived some harrowing experiences. Sometimes, the Gestapo would arrive unannounced. Looking for Jews and foreigners. Siegi and Stanko kept a sleeping bag by the door. Packed with some warm clothes and a cooker for food. If the Gestapo showed up, Stanko would grab the sleeping bag and head into the mountains for three days and nights. He would then return to the village after the Gestapo left. Most winter days were spent on the ski slopes. Siegi had skied with her grandmother since she was a child. Siegi and Stanko's eldest daughter, Petja, was born during their time in Garmisch. She started skiing when she was two.

The war finally ended. Germany was in ruins, as was much of the rest of Europe. Returning to law school was out of the picture for Stanko. Going back home to Bulgaria was likewise not an option. The future was America. Just as it was for my great-grandfather.

Stanko had kept in touch with his best childhood friend, Toshoff, who was in America. Toshoff was working for Radio Free Europe (RFE) out of New York. He suggested to Stanko that he, Siegi, and Petja come to New York. RFE had a job opening. So in 1951, the Gornev's arrived in New York. By 1954, the family had made a new addition: Ann. Soon to be called "Minky" after notoriously running around their house like a little mink. After a few years in Montclair, New Jersey, Stanko was transferred to the Washington, D.C. office and the Voice of America. The family of four relocated to the D.C. area and has been there ever since.

Chapter 10

Nasty Doubles

Everyone knows Nasty. Ilie "Nasty" Nastase was one of the greatest tennis players of all time. He won seven Grand Slam titles: two singles, three men's doubles, and two mixed doubles. The French Open, the U.S. Open, and the year-ending championships, known as the Masters Grand Prix, which has since been replaced with the Association of Tennis Professional (ATP) Tour World Championships. Ilie was ranked number one in the world in 1973 and 1974. Sure, Ilie came from a Communist satellite country, Romania, but Ilie didn't act like a Communist. He had personality. He had an outgoing personality. In addition to his seven Grand Slam titles, Ilie was in two memorable Wimbledon finals—one against Stan Smith in 1972, the other against Björn Borg in 1976.

I had played Ilie a number of times on the tour, and we sort of became friends. We didn't have dinner together or hang out, nothing like that. But we were friendly. And in

January 1979, at the WTC tournament in Richmond (also known as the United Virginia Bank Classic), he had my back, big time.

The tournament was played at the Richmond Coliseum. All the players were staying at the Richmond Hilton Hotel. Richmond is a cool town. The people there are great, and the tournament was sold out. Big tennis town. As it happened, my room at the hotel was directly across the hall from Nasty's.

On that Thursday afternoon, I was resting in my room. I was scheduled to play the first round doubles match later with Corrado Barazzutti of Italy against Brian Gottfried and John McEnroe, the tournament's third seed. We were scheduled for the last match of the day. The night session. Probably would not go on the court until at least 10:00 p.m. or later.

I'm lying on the bed in my room when I hear a lot of laughing and yelling outside my door. Whoever it is, they definitely aren't speaking English. I get up and open the door. Ilie and his Italian friend Bambino — who, I swear, looked exactly like Lucca Brasi from The Godfather — are horsing around in the hall. The door to Ilie's room is open.

Ilie sees me and yells out, "Hey, Vitz, what you doing?" I go into his room. Ilie jumps on the bed and stretches out, right next to Bambino, who's attempting to nap on the other side.

Ilie then turns on the TV and lies back down on the bed, propping up a couple of pillows so he can sit up. I sit down in a chair, and Nasty and I start rapping. He starts talking, of course, about the young woman who works at the front desk. He wants to know if I saw her today.

Then he says, "Hey, Vitz, you going to Florida next week?" There was a pretty big Association of Tennis Professional World Tour stop in Sarasota coming up. The ATP was founded in September 1972. In 1990, the ATP Tour era begins and a new tournament calendar was structured allowing for an eight-week off-season.

"Naw, Nasty," I say. "I didn't make it into that one. I'm about five spots out."

Nasty looks at me and nonchalantly asks, "Well, do you want to go?"

"Yeah," I say.

"Okay," says Nasty. "Bambino, wake up and get me that number of the guy in Florida."

Bambino gets up and starts looking around. But their room is not exactly clean. They had stuff all over the place. After about five minutes, Bambino still couldn't find anything. It was pathetic. So Nasty decided to join the hunt.

Finally, I say, "Hey man, don't worry about it. It's no

problem." Just then, Nasty holds up a piece of paper and says, "Here it is." He goes to the phone and dials the number on the piece of paper.

"Is Tom Cooke there?" Nasty says into the phone. "Can you tell him it's Nasty?" The next thing I hear Nasty say is, "Tom, things aren't looking good for coming down to Florida next week." There is a pause. Then Nasty continues, "My friend Steve Krulevitz is not in the draw so I can't make it." Another pause. Tom is likely panicking on the other end of the line and saying something like, "What do you mean, Steve Krulevitz, who?"

Nasty then says, "The only way I'm coming down is if Krulevitz gets a wild card into singles and we play doubles together."

Now I'm thinking, probably the same thing as Tom, What is going on here? Tom, surely in full-on panic mode by this point, must tell Nasty to hold the line because the next thing Nasty says is, "Make it fast 'cause I got to play soon." He had a second-round singles match against Jose Higueras of Spain.

A couple of long minutes later, Nasty hangs up the phone. Then he looks at me and says, "Hey, partner, make your flight to Florida."

***

It was a blast playing doubles with one of the greatest doubles player of all time, a guy who had won the French Open, with his countryman Ion Tiriac, the U.S. Open, with his buddy Jimmy Connors, and two Wimbledon mixed doubles titles, with American Rosemary Casals.

A total blast, that is, except for our first-round match, during which I, literally, for two sets missed 98 percent of my returns. Nasty and I were the third seed in the draw.

Nerves had me the whole match. Ilie was cool. "Don't worry, Vitz," he said. "Relax. I've got you." He carried us through. Played some intense doubles. The guy was a master, literally a genius. He knew where the ball was going before our opponents even hit it. Uncanny.

If you ever spent a week during a tour stop with Nasty, you know that he...well, he didn't exactly follow the basic training rules. Let's just say he packed a lot into a week. Now, I'm not saying the girl from the front desk of the Richmond Hilton had something to do with his busy off-court schedule in Sarasota. But I'm not saying she didn't either. With Nasty, you never knew.

So here we are. The day of the doubles final. Ilie first has to play his singles semifinal match against Rick Meyer, an unseeded American who is having the tournament of his life. Nasty starts off well, but the week is catching up to him. He goes down, 6-2 in the third.

We're scheduled to play in the doubles final next. I head down to the locker room and find Ilie slouched down in a corner. Not looking very fresh or eager to play any more tennis.

"Hey man, bad luck," I say. "The good news is, I'm feeling it today. I got you covered."

Ilie looks up at me and says, "Tell them I'll be ready in ten minutes."

I have to say, without a doubt, and no conceit, I played the best doubles match of my life that day. Ilie didn't even play fifty percent of his capacity. But it didn't matter. I played one hundred and fifty percent of mine.

We took the title in two sets, 7-6, 6-3.

The tour can be a lonely place. Guys aren't falling all over each other to help one another out. It's an individual sport. You're out there on your own. Sure, with doubles it's a little different. But even then, your partner today could be your opponent in singles tomorrow. Dog eat dog. Cutthroat. That's the tour.

Ilie was thirty-two years old and ranked number sixteen in the world when we played that tournament together in Sarasota. He had a lot more tennis and several more titles to come, but his best days on the court were behind him, and he knew it. He had no reason to do me that favor, to get me into that tournament and play doubles with me. Other than the fact, I guess, that he liked me. And because he felt like doing it. And because he could do it.

After the match, we drove back to the Town of Longboat Key together. Sometimes life on the tour can be pretty sweet.

Chapter 11

Mind Freeze in Finland

I had declared myself professional in 1973 at twenty-two. A dream come true. Now it's June 1982 and the end of the line is rapidly approaching. I'm thirty-one and in the twilight. My ranking is dropping. I had come up to Tampere Tennis Center in Finland to get some ATP computer points. The computer ranking system was first introduced by the ATP on August 23, 1973, with Ilie Nastase becoming the first number one.

Tampere is a two-hour train ride north from Helsinki. The Tampere Open, part of the ATP Challenger Tour, is being played during the second week of the French Open. Total prize money is $25,000. $5,000 to the winner and $2,500 to the runner-up. Cash.

Weller Evans, the ATP tour manager, brought this Finnish tournament to my attention. "Hey, Vitz," he said. "If you don't make it to the second week of the French, there's a tournament that you might want to consider up in Finland.

You should enter, just in case."

Smart call by Weller. Seeing as how I wasn't exactly a regular in singles the second week of Grand Slams, it was a good idea. Weller was a Princeton graduate, a guy who'd played briefly on the tour and knew the ropes. He was the man. On Weller's advice, I didn't enter the doubles in Paris. Even if I don't make it to the second week of the French, my ranking is good enough for direct entry into Tampere. I'd never been that far north. Man, it's definitely different up there in Finland.

I'm the third seed in the tournament. In the first two rounds, I roll through Bill Cowan of Canada, and Magnus Tideman of Sweden. In the quarterfinals, I'm up against Christoph Zipf, a West German, who is eleven years younger than I am.

Suddenly, I didn't have any feel. Blame it on the Finnish clay. Whatever it was I was down, 6-7, 0-3, and completely frustrated. It wasn't because I was losing. It was because of how I was playing. Sure, Zipf was making me play lousy, but it was more than just him.

At 3-0 for Zipf in the second set, my serve at 30-40. Break point. Lose this and it will be 7-6, 4-0, Zipf. If that happens the curtains will come out. I serve to his backhand. He hits the return down the line to my forehand. And I still can't believe to this day what I did next. I changed my grip from an Eastern grip to a Continental grip, or service grip—got underneath the ball and with a badminton type swing popped the ball 500 feet straight up in the air on my side of the court. I cracked. Tanked. 4-0, Zipf. Embarrassing. Humiliating.

I walk over to my chair, dig in my bag, and grab a different racquet. I ping the strings with my left hand. Take a deep breath and walk out to return Zipf's serve—Zipf, without a doubt, is now thinking, Who do I play my semifinal match against?

Zipf serves. I hit a big return. He hits it back. I put the forehand away. Bury it. The shot feels good. Now I'm swinging hard, and everything starts going in. Like magic. I break his serve. My serve starts to click. Easy service hold.

I'm one break down when Zipf wakes up, and then the dance begins. Now I'm hitting the ball heavier than before but I'm not missing. Plus, my legs start feeling like a twenty-two year old's. Hey, I'm starting to like the North Country.

Zipf starts thinking. I can tell. That's bad for a tennis player. Thinking wrong thoughts. When the wrong thoughts pop in your head, you're in trouble. You have maybe ten to twelve seconds between points. That's when you don't want to think. You want to visualize. Those ten seconds can be like five minutes if you're thinking the wrong thoughts. Thoughts can grow like weeds or bloom like beautiful flowers. If Zipf is thinking, then those thoughts are going to translate into his game. And I had a hunch that was exactly what was going on. Guten tag, mein freund — which is German for "Good day my friend."

It's four-all, and I'm digging this comeback. Finally playing some good tennis but, more importantly, I'm enjoying the battle. Zipf holds serve and goes up 5-4. I play a really good game, but he comes up with the goods. On the changeover, I'm positive. I'm playing really well. I'm not thinking that if I lose my serve, it's over. No way. I'm not thinking at all. I'm visualizing. How am I going to play the first point of the next game? I go through it in my mind. Play it out in my head while I sit in my changeover chair.

Then I'm up and out there. It's a dogfight. Zipf goes up match point, 30-40. I'm waiting for the ball from the ball boy, but I'm focusing on hitting my serve hard and down the middle. I take my time. I'm not ready to stop playing now. Breathe, Vitz. Relax. Take your time. I do. And then, bam! Down the middle, with pace. Zipf barely gets his racquet on the ball. Deuce. I win the game. Now it's five-all. Then, it's 6-5, Zipf. That's fine.

My serve now. At 15-30, Zipf attacks the net. Good play. He's trying to earn the W. Make a volley or two at a crucial point in the match and you deserve to win. You've earned it. Most players, when they're closing in on a victory, hang on the baseline, hoping their opponent will make a couple of mistakes. Some unenforced errors. Wrong thinking, again. When you're behind in tennis, you've got to fight harder. You've got to concentrate better. But when you're up in tennis, you tend to let down a bit. That's human nature.

Zipf comes to the net trying to earn himself another match point. I rip a backhand shot crosscourt and Zipf hits a beautiful volley down the line. I'm sure he thinks it's a winner. But somehow I get there and throw up a lob that's not too short but not real deep either. Zipf is a little slow getting back, but it's an overhead he has hit 5,000 times and made 4,995 times. I struggle to recover. The court is wide open. Zipf lines up his overhead and hits it two feet beyond the baseline. Unbelievable. First rule of tennis: Always make your opponent hit another shot. Zipf, not surprisingly, cracks in the tiebreaker, and we're knotted at one set apiece. To Zipf's credit, he rebounds in the third. Now we're both playing really well. It's tight. Somehow I eke out another tiebreak by the skin of my teeth.

Honestly, there were two little seeds of doubt that got sewn in Zipf's mind — the first is when he blew the 4-0 lead he had in the second set, and the second is when he missed the overhead that would have given him a double match point, plus he had another match point at 5-4 in the second set — might have been what made the difference in the end. Thinking the wrong thoughts is deadly. Never let anyone tell you tennis isn't a mental game.

In the semifinals, I'm up against the top seed, Stanislaw Berner, from Czechoslovakia. Berner is five years younger than I am and ranked number 60 in the world. He gets a lot of balls back and fights like a tiger. I'm hitting big. My serve is clicking. My forehand, too. I'm hitting winners on clay. I crush him, 6-3, 6-3.

The final is on Sunday and being covered by National Finnish TV. Leo Palin of Finland is doing the TV. He'd just lost in the doubles quarterfinals of the French and came up to do the commentary for the final.

It's a warm day with a bright blue sky. I'm playing Peter Bastiansen from Denmark. A guy who is eleven years younger than I am, and playing in only the second challenger event of his life.

I'm playing well. But so is he. Good final. Good tennis. I win the first set, 6-3. Then, in the second set at 5-4, I reach match point, 40-30. My legs are still feeling young. But, all of a sudden, my mind freezes and starts functioning like a ninety-one year old's. I'm rushing which is a huge mistake. I want to win so badly. I want to hold up that trophy. I don't slow down. I serve too quickly. I'm choking.

During the next rally, Bastiansen slices his backhand crosscourt and comes to the net for the first time in two sets. The ball is low. I slice back crosscourt, and he pops up a volley. It drops at the service line, right at mid-court. There it is. Five grand. Sitting right there. I start to go for it, but my legs won't move. I finally get to the ball. It's truly an easy pass. But I hit it right into the net.

What a choke. Horrible choke. I can't believe it. I'm cracking, falling apart, mentally. I've lost my mojo. I'm so pissed. Bastiansen wins the set, 7-5. Then he takes the title, 6-2, in the third.

The tournament is over. I can't believe it, but it's for real. I've lost. I'm in tears but trying to hide it. I will never be the 1982 Tampere Open Champion. Long awards ceremony. No interview with Palin. Well, that's tennis. That's life. And as Mick Jagger would say, "You can't always get what you want."

***

"Can you ring my room tomorrow at 7:00 a.m., please?" I ask the switchboard clerk at Hotel Tampere. The hotel is directly across the street from the train station. My train doesn't leave until tomorrow morning at 9:00 a.m. Two hours south to Helsinki. Grab a taxi from the train station. One-hour ride to the airport. My non-stop flight to Venice, Italy is at 2:45 p.m. In the first round, I'm scheduled to play Bruce Derlin from New Zealand. The winner of that match plays Panatta on Center court, for sure.

I ask the guy behind the desk for the key. "Four twenty-seven," I say. I head up to my room. It's 6:10 p.m. on Sunday night. Man, it's so quiet. I mean, there's nobody around. It's like everyone just left. The lobby is empty and so is the fourth floor. All week long, the hotel was jumping. There is not a soul in sight. This is so strange. Where did everyone go? Has the plague hit?

I phone Ann, who is my wife now, from my room. She's already at the Excelsior in Venice, waiting for me. I tell her a little about the match but, more importantly, "I can't wait to see you tomorrow. I should be at the hotel around 6:00 p.m. We'll get some dinner," I say. Then I hang up. I wish I was leaving tonight. I pack up a few things and head out to get something to eat. I'm starving.

Tennis players are superstitious. Most athletes are.

We travel every week to a different city. Stay at different a hotel. Eat at a different restaurant. So when we find that one restaurant outside the States that's good, we have a tendency

140

to go back. Every night. Especially if we don't get sick in the middle of the night. Superstition. Let me put it this way there are some great restaurants in Paris. The best in the world. So every night, I eat at the Etoile Verte. Why take a chance, right?

So I'm back at the same restaurant in Tampere. I found it the day I arrived. Now seven days later I'm still eating there. It's working. I'm the only one still in town out of the thirty-two singles players, plus the doubles guys. Bastiansen drove from Copenhagen. He had his car at the tennis club. Leo Palin took off after the doubles final. I've got the $2,500 in my pocket. Good dinner. I needed it.

Back at the hotel, I check in with the clerk. He's in his late thirties. "You have me down for a 7:00 a.m. wakeup call, right?" I ask him.

"Sure," he says. "7:00 a.m."

"Thanks. Can I have my key, it's 427. Also, I'm going to pay my bill now. I made a phone call about an hour and a half ago," I say.

I finish packing and set the $2,500 cash on the counter top of the dresser. Lock the door. Set my alarm just in case the hotel screws up. Can't miss that train. I lie down. Very tired, long week, and I'm out.

BANG! BANG! BANG!

Someone is knocking on my door. Wow. What's going on? I look at my watch next to the bed. It's 2:41 in the morning. The banging gets more intense. "Open the door!" someone yells from outside. "Open the door! Emergency! Open the door!" Then more banging.

It's still twilight outside. Not dark. I slowly get up. Someone is turning the doorknob. "Wait a minute!" I yell out.

"Open the door!" the man yells again. "Emergency!"

I walk toward the door. It's a big wooden Scandinavian door. There is no peephole. Just a big wooden door. I reach to open it, but for some reason, I stop. "Who's there?" I call out.

"It's the hotel manager, now open the door immediately!"

"What's the matter?" I ask. I'm becoming more and more awake now.

"It's an emergency," another male voice says.

Two guys. Not good. The doorknob jiggles again. I walk quickly over to the room phone and dial 0. After about ten rings, I hang up.

I'm wide awake now. Wide awake. I reach for my racquet bag sitting on the chair and pull out two Prince Graphite racquets.

So there I am standing in the middle of a hotel room in

Tampere, Finland, holding a graphite tennis racquet in each hand, scared shitless. My pulse is 220, for sure. I can still hear the guys outside the door, and it's tense, really tense. I'm standing there for what seems like an eternity. I put one racquet down and dial 0 again. I hang up after thirty rings this time. Still no answer. Right then, I hear a car start up in the alley, outside my window. Then I hear it drive away.

***

I know from having my first match of this tournament scheduled for 9:00 a.m. that the hotel breakfast room opens at 6:00 a.m. during the week. Always get up three hours before your match. If you play at 8:00 a.m., wakeup time is 5:00 a.m. I know this from my junior days.

It's 6:02 a.m. and I'm in the breakfast room at the Tampere Hotel. At 6:45 a.m. I'm buying a ticket for the 7:00 a.m. train from Tampere to Helsinki. I know the train runs every hour during the week.

I arrive early at the Helsinki Airport, but who cares. It's the tour. Hurry up and wait. At least here there aren't any big wooden Scandinavian doors for people to pound on.

On Tuesday, I take care of Bruce Derlin from New Zealand. Wednesday, in the late afternoon, I'm on Center court in Venice. Italian TV is covering Adriano Panatta in the second round of the Venice Open. I'd say I was "safe and sound," except that a non-Italian tennis player is never safe or sound when he's playing an Italian in front of psychotic Italian tennis fans. Especially if that Italian happens to be Panatta, who is basically a god of mythological stature in his home country.

Thankfully, the fans in Venice aren't nearly as rabid as the ones in Rome. I take Panatta out in three sets. No one throws any rotten fruit or coins at me. I'm up against Jimmy Brown in the quarterfinals. He is a young American kid from Florida. Only seventeen years old. In his previous match, he had knocked off Jose Higueras of Spain, the third seed. I take the first set off him, 2-6, but he gets the next two.

On to the doubles. My partner, David Carter of Australia, and I are seeded third. We make it to the semis, going down, 7-6, 6-3, to the second seed, Carlos Kirmayr and Cassio Motta of Brazil. Too bad. Could have played against my old partner Nastase if we had made it to the final.

Wimbledon starts in two weeks.

Chapter 12

U.S. Open

Ninety-nine percent of all professional tennis players would tell you that if they could win one tennis tournament it would be Wimbledon. The big "W" is the top tournament. No doubt. But for me, I would take the U.S. Open.

The U.S. Open is the modern day version of the United States National Tennis Championships, which was founded in 1881 and is one of the oldest tennis tournaments in the world.

The U.S. Open, which is held annually, starts on the final Monday in August, and lasts for two weeks into September. The middle weekend coincides with the Labor Day holiday weekend. This hard court tennis tournament is held in the greatest city in the world — New York.

From 1881 to 1914, the tournament was held on grass courts at the Newport Casino in Newport, Rhode Island. In its first few years, only members of the USNLTA were permitted to enter the tournament. Richard Sears was the first player to win the tournament. From 1884 to 1911, the tournament used a challenge system whereby the defending champion would automatically qualify for next year's final in which he would play the winner of the All-Comers event.

In 1915, the U.S. National Tennis Championships relocated to Forest Hills, New York at the West Side Tennis Club. From 1921 to 1923, the tournament was played at the Germantown Cricket Club in Philadelphia. The tournament returned to Forest Hills in 1924, following the building of a 14,000 seat outdoor tennis stadium.

During the first few years of the U.S. National Tennis Championships, the tournament was known as the U.S. National Singles Championships for Men and only men were allowed to compete. Six years later in 1887, the first official U.S. Women's National Singles Championships was held at the Philadelphia Cricket Club, the oldest country club in the United States.

The U.S. Open era began in 1968 when the tournament was renamed the United States Open Tennis Championships. That year the tournament was open to professionals for the first time and 96 men and 63 women entered the event. The prize money totaled $100,000.

Since 1987, the U.S. Open has been chronologically the

fourth and final tennis major comprising the Grand Slam each year. The other three majors, in chronological order, are the Australian Open, the French Open, and Wimbledon.

Most of my memories go back to the West Side Tennis Club. In 1964, I won the boys' 14-and-under Eastern Sectional Championships. I even stayed at the Forest Hills Hotel by myself for the whole week. In today's world, no parent would even consider that.

The Eastern Sectional Championships were played on the club's clay courts which surrounded the grass courts. So you could say I had an unfair advantage at the 1970's qualifying rounds for the U.S. Open. How I got into the qualifying was a mystery.

I had won two matches and I am now playing a senior from the University of California, Berkeley for a spot in the U.S. National Tennis Championships. The first set was ugly but I am hanging tight in the second. After fighting off a couple of match points at 4-5 we are now in a nine-point tiebreaker. This is different from today's twelve-point system, where you have to win by two. From 1970 to 1974, the tournament used a best-of-nine point, sudden death tiebreaker. The tiebreaker back in the day was first to five points, so it was called the nine-pointer. I would serve two points and then my opponent would serve two points. I serve another two and my opponent serves the last three. On the ninth and deciding point, the receiver has their choice of which side they want to return from. I'm down 4-1 in the tiebreaker. Pretty much curtains. But then I remember my opponent becoming very nervous. He double faults twice and I win the tiebreaker, 5-4 and on to the main draw of the U.S. Open.

And who do I draw in the first round? Some guy from Romania named, Ilie Nastase. He is the seventh seed. We are on court number nine. The only problem is Nastase is nowhere to be found. He never made the trip across the big pond to the United States and is somewhere still in Europe. So a lucky loser goes into the main draw. (A lucky loser is the highest ranked player who has lost in the final round of a qualifying match and enters the main draw of the tournament.)

My next match is against a guy from India which isn't necessarily a good thing for me. In India they tend to play a lot of grass court tennis and the main draw is on grass. I go down 6-4 in the fifth set.

In 1971, I qualify to get into the U.S. Open qualifying, which is being played on hard courts at the Port Washington Tennis Academy in Long Island, New York. A couple of days before I practice with my buddy Steve Turner on the clay courts in mid-town Manhattan, which really pays off. I beat Mike Estep from Texas in the first-round at the U.S. Open, 6-4 in the fifth. It's a big win for me. My celebration is crushed by a guy you may have heard of named Arthur Ashe. Ashe shows me that I have a long way to go in developing my grass game.

In 1972, I'm confident. I am playing Wanaro N'Godrella from France. I ask around but no one has heard of the guy. I lose in four sets. N'Godrella goes on to win another match after me but eventually loses to the eleventh seed Cliff Drysdale from South Africa in four close sets. The following year N'Godrella beats the 1975 U.S. Open winner Manuel Orantes in the second round of the singles at the French Open.

I'm back again in the qualifying in 1973. I have a good run and make it to the main draw. This year I'm pumped. I have something to prove. I draw thirty-two year old Pierre Barthès. I am only twenty-two years old. Barthès was one of the Handsome Eight (a collection of players who were signed by Lamar Hunt in 1968 to play in the newly formed World Championship Tennis series). The World Championship Tennis (WCT), established in 1968, was the tour for professional male tennis players. I had no idea that Barthès had won the 1970 U.S. National Doubles Championships on grass at the West Side Tennis Club with his partner, Nikola

"Niki" Pilić, from Yugoslavia (another member of the Handsome Eight). I lose a close first set, 6-4, and win the second, 6-3. I'm feeling pretty good on the grass court but then the rug gets pulled from under me and I go down, 6-1, 6-2.

In 1974, I have enough ATP points to go straight into the main draw. The U.S. Open has a main draw of 128 players of which sixteen spots are reserved for qualifiers and seven for wild cards. I got straight into the main draw of the tournament only to lose first round to the eleventh seed, Marty Riessen. But the kicker is that I was actually up two sets to love on the clubhouse court and playing great before Riessen came back and destroyed me in the last three sets. 6-0 in the fifth still hurts to this day. Big, big win, not to be. In September 1974, Riessen reaches his highest ATP singles ranking of number 11 in the world.

In 1975, I am in the U.S. Open main draw and play my UCLA teammate Jeff Austin. Jeff is also the older brother of John and Tracy Austin. John and Tracy won the 1980 Wimbledon mixed doubles together and became the first brother and sister to win a Grand Slam title. I start out too fast, winning the first set, 6-3. By the second set my energy drops about three levels. I lose the second set, 4-6, but am up 3-1 in the third. As each game goes by I feel worse and worse. I end

150

up losing 3-6 in the third. Tough loss. That same year, I sign with adidas and I'm provided with some of the best tennis gear around.

In 1976, I have my best year yet on the tour. I am in the main draw of the U.S. Open and play one of my best matches. I beat Balazs Taroczy from Hungary, 7-6, 7-5. Balazs Taroczy reached a career-high singles ranking of number nine in the world. After five long years of drought at my favorite tournament I finally have won a match. But then I run into Vytautas "Vitas" Gerulaitis, who is the sixteenth seed. He destroys me 6-2, 6-2.

I am back in the main draw for the seventh year in a row. First round, I take down the South African David Schneider, 6-4, 6-3. Next, I go up against Adriano Panetta of Italy. I wish I could have this one back. I go down 6-1, 7-6. Never really felt good hitting the ball during that match. Obviously, Adriano had something to do with that.

The week before the U.S. Open I arrive in Boston after playing a tournament in Stowe, Vermont, which had followed another tournament that I played in Indiana. I play the U.S. Pro Tennis Championships in Chestnut Hill, Massachusetts, just outside of Boston at the Longwood Cricket Club and beat Alvaro Fillol from Chile, 6-4, 7-5.

After the match I call Ann and tell her about it. "Yeah, I

beat Fillol in two sets," I say. "It looks like I'll play Adriano Panatta from Italy on Wednesday if he wins his match tonight." Panatta had won the '76 Italian and French Opens.

"Good luck," she says. "My birthday is on Wednesday."

"I'm going to beat him as your birthday present," I say. Macho man like.

Ann is turning twenty four. I'm twenty seven. On Wednesday morning, I head down to the lobby of the Holiday Inn in Newton for some breakfast. I step out of the elevator and sitting right there in front of me is Ann. She's wearing jeans and a white tank top. Nice jeans and a sexy white tank top. She looks unbelievable. *What a good-looking German-Bulgarian girl*, I think. I doubt anyone in the history of the world has ever worn a tank top as well as her.

That morning she had gotten up at 4:30 a.m., taken a 6:00 a.m. flight from D.C. to Boston, grabbed a taxi, and arrived at the hotel all by 8:30 a.m. Panatta, that poor guy, had zero chance in this match. I crush him, 6-2, 6-4.

"So where should I take you for your birthday dinner?" I ask Ann after the match.

"Wherever you want," she says. Then I realize something. I know just the spot.

"Do you like seafood?" I ask. "Boston has some of the best

152

seafood around. Have you ever been to Fenway Park?"

"No," Ann says. "Never been!"

Next up, I play Arthur Ashe. This time he teaches me that I have a long way to go in developing my clay court game.

From the end of 1977 and into the early part of 1978, I had a nagging case of tennis elbow. My ranking went south and I didn't have enough points for the main draw. Even though I was starting to play well again that summer with a win over Adriano Panatta, who beat me the previous year at the U.S. Open, I lose in the last round of the 1978 qualifying in three tight sets to Trey Waltke from St. Louis, Missouri.

You know that expression, "You ain't getting any younger." That's a direct remark about your joints. When you are young, you think nothing of making sudden start and stop movements. But as you get older, you realize that your body is not as flexible as it used to be. Your body starts talking to you, and you better listen.

Your body is not properly prepared for the rigors of the pro tour. Little injuries crop into your training and then your matches. You heal slower. You lose valuable practice time. You lose confidence in your body.

One sudden movement, one twist or turn, in the wrong direction can result in injury. Even coming back too soon could cause more injury. What happens when you do come back and you lose? What does that do for your confidence? Other players hear you've been out because of an injury. That makes them hang on longer against you; they purposefully wear you down. They're more confident and doubt themselves less. Pretty soon it's over.

In 1979, I was back in the main draw of the U.S. Open. I take out the Frenchman, Patrice Dominguez in short order. Only to fall 6-2 in the fifth to Butch Walts after leading two sets to one. I'm liking the hard courts at Flushing Meadows but hating the heat and humidity. I vowed 1980 would be better.

In 1980, I defeat Andrew Pattison of Rhodesia in the first round of the main draw in four tough sets. Pattison's career high singles ATP ranking was number 24 in the world. This was big because I had not been doing much at the U.S. Open in the best of five set matches. Next, I get the grandstand against John McEnroe. It was a great first set. I'm up a set point in the tie breaker but McEnroe picks it up and takes care of me pretty easily in the next two sets.

I'm back in the main draw of the U.S. Open in 1981. In the first round, I play Francisco Gonzalez from Puerto Rico. I am up two sets to love but lose the third, 2-6. I cannot let this happen again. So in the fourth I give it all I've got and take it

7-5. In the next round, I lose to my longtime friend from the juniors, Dick Stockton, in three straight sets.

Once again I am back in 1982 for my twelfth and last main draw match in the U.S. Open. I take the first set from the Brazilian Marcos Hocevar. Only to go down in four easy sets.

In the spring of 1983, I play in an ATP $25,000 challenger event. I'm at the Galatina Tennis Club. The weather is very nice down in the boot—no rain, dry, low humidity, if any. It's sunny and pretty hot in Europe. A perfect day for playing tennis on red clay.

"Hey Steve," says Shahar Perkiss, the former Israeli Davis Cup star, who reached a career-high singles ranking of number 53 in the world. Shahar is 6'4" and weighs 150 pounds.

I look up at him and am blinded by the sun. "Manish ma?" I ask. —which is Hebrew for "How are you?"

"Doing pretty well," Shahar says. Shahar is from Haifa, Israel. He has a big, big serve and one hell of a forehand. "I want you to check out these guys practicing," Shahar says to me.

I follow Shahar over to the practice courts. The first guy I notice has an incredible kick serve. I remember thinking to myself he's amazing. It turns out to be Stefan Edberg. The next guy I see hitting has a two-hand backhand. Also incredible. It's Miloslav Mecir from Slovakia.

"Look there Steve, those two are brothers," Shahar says, pointing to Emilio and Javier Sanchez from Spain. They are only fifteen and seventeen years old. They're incredible.

I watch all three courts for a few minutes. "These guys will be top ten in the next five years," I say. "That's why I am retiring this year or next."

Shahar looks down at me and says, "Does Shlomie know?" Shahar is talking about former Israeli Davis Cup player Shlomo Glickstein and one of my best friends on the tour. In November of 1982, Shlomo reached a career-high singles ranking of number 22 in the world.

Feeling somewhat guilty, I say, "I haven't seen him for a few months, but hopefully we'll get to catch up sometime soon." Over dinner that night and some very good linguini with clam sauce, I'm ready to retire from the tour.

Later that year in the 1983 U.S. Open, I lose in the second round of the qualifying in straight sets to the same guy from the year before, Hocevar. The writing is on the wall. I'm thirty-two years old. Eleven great years competing on the men's professional ATP tour. Not bad. It's time to pick up another profession. It's time to become a U.S. Open spectator.

Chapter 13

TFT

We are leaving on the six o'clock train tomorrow morning out of Long Island for New York City. I am staying at Peter Jeffers' house. It's during the 1982 United States Open Tennis Championships, held right down the road in Flushing Meadows-Corona Park. You know the place — the USTA Billie Jean King National Tennis Center. Peter works on Wall Street. He has his own firm. He is very smart and wants to teach me the business inside and out. This could be a big future for me. So I check it out.

I'm up at 5:00 a.m. to catch the 6:20 a.m. train to the office. I spend the day trading and learning. I am back home at 7:45 p.m. It's only Tuesday. Still have three days left in the week. Peter sometimes goes into the office for a few hours on Saturday.

I know I can't play tennis forever, no one can. No one can travel every week. You just can't. So it's time to decide my future. Do I want to teach tennis for a living like Maury Schwartzman and Glenn Bassett? Do I want to start a tennis program or academy like Nick Bollettieri did in Florida and develop some of my own players? Maybe Maury can help me get started. Maybe a few old competitors like Tim Mayotte, Colin Dibley, Harold Solomon, and Ilie Nastase will come and play some exhibitions at my tennis academy.

***

When you come off the pro tour at thirty-two years old, let's face it, what skills do you have? I mean, all you've ever done since the age of eight is hit tennis balls.

What are you qualified for? Well, there's tennis. And then there is, um…tennis.

You know what's sad? You can't even get a job at a country club as the head pro or the director. Do you know why? No experience. The tennis committee doesn't want to risk hiring you. What if you don't like brown-nosing the members at the club and you quit. The committee has to meet again and go through the entire process all over. So, it's better to hire someone with "experience."

So where does that leave me? Where does that leave the guy who didn't make the big bucks? The guy who paid $90,000 in cash for a townhouse, and bought two used Volvos from Tony Hines in New Jersey, along with a couple of sofas, and a few TVs. I'll tell you where that leaves you. It leaves you with a balance in the checking account of $8,500. And married. It's not just you, but you have a wife to take care of. That's ten years on the road. Grinding.

Most of the time I was on the tour I was based in California. As my ranking improved, I decided to relocate back east. I needed an airport that was easily accessible to Europe since I was traveling there three or four times a year. California was another five hours on the plane. Too far.

I had a company drive my Pontiac Firebird to Maryland. I parked it at my parents' house on Claran Road in Baltimore. Occasionally, our neighbor Ivan Feit would appear at the door. "Is Steve in town? I have a nine year old son who's a pretty good tennis player. I would love if Steve could hit with him." My parents were under strict instructions to say I was not around. I was on the road. Even if I was actually home. I'm not around, period. Except that day I ran into Ivan outside in front of my parents' house. I'm going to be thirty-three in a few months. Off the tour. And looking at options.

I'd just spoken that week to Peter Jeffers from Long Island, New York. He wanted me to move there and travel into Wall Street every morning on the 7:00 a.m. with him. Take the Long Island Railroad. Wear a suit and tie, every day.

I didn't know about that. I'm a tracksuit kind of guy. My necktie knots never turn out well. I'm better off in tennis gear. Why? Because I love tennis. But more importantly because I've got experience in tennis, not the financial stock market in the Big Apple.

"Hi, Steve," Ivan says. "Do you have any time to hit with Ricky? He's now eleven and a pretty darn good player."

"Sure Ivan," I say. Why not? What else do I have to do? "Let me see if I can get a court somewhere." *Maybe Bare Hills Tennis Club*, I think.

Maury Schwartzman was over at Bare Hills (yes that's the Maury who taught me tennis). He was the premier pro at the Club so they had a special teaching court just for him.

I would sit on the side for hours and watch Maury teach lesson after lesson. I soaked in a lot of knowledge listening to him. And, of course, don't forget the Pikesville Library. I checked out every book on tennis and teaching tennis that I could find. I did my homework, and it paid off. Ricky progressed. Got to the finals of the Maryland State Championships. Pretty soon, Sol "The King" Schwartz, Marc "The Mean Lean Guy" Kolodner, Chris "The Hulk" Santos, and Marc "The Beetle" Baylin all wanted lessons. Man was I busy. Not long after that, I had my own business going: The Steve Krulevitz Tennis Program. For a logo I use the five-ball logo from the 1984 Summer Olympics but with tennis balls in a pyramid shape, to represent the Harry Hopman five-ball drill—a brutal, five-ball pickup, sprint drill.

It turned out my high school guidance counselor hadn't been so wrong after all. I had learned a trade and that trade was tennis. The pro tour had been my ten-year apprenticeship. Now I was a master. And it was time to pass on what I had learned through the years to others. Maybe even a pro player.

"Steve. It's Jerry Solomon," says Jerry.

"Hey, Jerry. What's going on?" I ask him.

Jerry Solomon is working for ProServ. ProServ has more athletes and clients than any other firm in the country. At its peak, ProServ represented more than two hundred professional athletes and coaches, including Michael Jordan, Patrick Ewing, and Jimmy Connors. The firm also managed and promoted professional sporting events and created ProServ television to handle sports production. Jerry was one of ProServ's top sports agents from 1980 to 1993. In 1994, Jerry started StarGames LLC, a sports marketing, management, and entertainment company, based outside of Boston. StarGames represents current and former athletes, including Jerry's wife, Nancy Kerrigan, a former American figure skater and two-time Olympic medalist, and Ivan Lendl, a tennis legend who was number one in the world.

When I came off the tour in early '84, I called ProServ and told Jerry to keep my number on file because I was looking for some pro players to coach. Now, five years later in February of 1989, I get the call.

"Listen, Steve, I've got this kid Jaime Yzaga. Twenty-one years old. He's been through three coaches. The kid has a lot of talent. Would you be interested in working with him?" Jerry asks me.

Truthfully, I'd never heard of Jaime Yzaga. I knew he was from a South American country. But I couldn't tell you which one.

"Sure Jerry. Let's do it," I say.

I wanted to coach a player on the pro tour and here was my chance. What was there to think about? Keep it simple.

"He has a place in Key Biscayne," Jerry says. "I want you to go there for a week and you guys work together. See how it goes. But let me talk to him first."

Jerry tells me Jaime is currently ranked number 86 in the world. Jaime will be in Miami the beginning of February and wants me to come down there.

"No problem, Jerry," I say. "I'm available. Let me know."

The weather in Miami is nice in February. The winter on the East Coast and the cold gets old. Early February in Key Biscayne is a good break.

Jerry calls again. "Steve, it's all set," he says.

"That's cool, Jerry," I say. "Give me Jaime's number at his place in Key Biscayne. I'll call him with my arrival time."

This is important. I want Jaime to pick me up at the airport. Right off the bat this establishes a certain sense of commitment. I can tell on our initial phone call that Jaime isn't too thrilled with this idea. But I have to set the parameters.

My flight gets in around dinnertime. I tell Jaime to meet me at the baggage claim and we'll grab a quick bite. While eating dinner at a local restaurant in Key Biscayne, I say to Jaime, "Look, I've got a wife and young daughter at home. I've also got a business; I'm running my own business. I work seven days a week." I'm not bragging or looking for a round of applause here. I just want this kid to understand that I have a life. I don't want to waste my time or his time. "I'm a professional," I say. "I'm not along for the ride."

Jaime's not sure what to make of me. I can tell. I can also tell that this is an intelligent guy sitting across the table from me. I doubt his other coaches talked to him like this.

"Sure, I want to work and coach on the pro level," I go on.

"It's a high level, and I'm used to it. But I'm going to be away from home, from family, and from the business I've built. I'm not into screwing that up."

I let that sink in for a second before I continue. "The tour is hard," I say. "I know. I've been out there. But if we stick together, good things can happen."

We set our first practice for the next morning at ten o'clock. "But," I tell Jaime, "we have to get up at 8:00 a.m. because at 9:15 a.m. we're going to warm up before we practice." Jaime looks surprised. "When we get to the court that we have reserved for ten o'clock, I want your body to be ready," I say. "Also make sure to bring a couple of extra shirts to change into." This kid is going to work like he's never worked before in his life.

Jaime is short. Solomon-sized. He has a beautiful one-handed backhand that generates pace and a slice he mixes in for variety. I'm stunned, however, that he's not serving with a full Continental grip. I can't believe this. He doesn't hit his volleys with Continental either. Ditto for his overhead. His forehand is also a bit sloppy. He has some holes in his game, no question. But he has good hands. And the holes in his game really only require small adjustments. I tell him he can make those adjustments, absolutely, and in a short amount time.

Our first practice together lasts two hours. Jaime works hard. He starts to make adjustments on his grips right away. Always listen to your coach. The kid is already showing that he's coachable. He wants to improve. He listens. This could be the start of something. We change our shirts and head out to get some lunch.

Over lunch, just as during dinner the evening before, I'm honest with him. "I like the way you hit the ball," I say. "Your strokes are solid. But we have to make some small adjustments on your volleys and serve. No big deal. I know you're ranked eighty-six right now. But I think you can do way better."

I ask the waitress for an extra pen. I take my napkin and write down: 19. I slide the napkin over to Jaime. "There it is," I say. "That's your goal. Number 19 in the world by the fall. By the end of the French Open, Wimbledon, and the U.S. Open."

I let Jaime chew on that for a second. "So how do we get there?" I say. "We work professionally and put our energy into obtaining this ranking. We need to improve our endurance, strength, technique, and tactics."

On the napkin I write down: T-F-T (Technique. Fitness. Tactics).

There's no way around it; we have to improve his strategy. Jaime's small. He doesn't have the reach at the net or the height for overheads. So when he comes to the net, he can't volley deep or he'll get passed or lobbed. He'll be like a sitting duck. So we work on short angle volleys. He can handle this, I know, because he has soft hands. Excellent touch.

Another thing: Jaime likes to come into the net crosscourt on too many of his approach shots. Opens the court right up. Makes it tougher on himself. We have to get him coming in down the line more often. He also needs to get fitter. We do more ball pick-up sprints on the court, and some off the court weight training too.

Jaime likes organization. He doesn't like surprises. I adjust Jaime's schedule. We go hour by hour. Get up, eat breakfast, warm-up on the track, not at the courts. That way, when we get to the courts to hit or practice with another pro player, we're all ready to go. Oh yes, and when I say we, I mean I'm doing the training, the warm-up, and the weights right alongside him. I live for this.

Getting a massage also becomes a must. Every day a massage for one hour. Then over to Fort Lauderdale twice a week to visit with a sports psychologist. The same sports psychologist Ivan Lendl uses.

N-I-N-E-T-E-E-N

I start to become obsessed with the number 19, and I make Jaime obsessed with it too. I write it on his grips, his bag. On the refrigerator in his apartment. Just the number "19," that's it.

We talk over his schedule. Not just today, but for the entire year. Have to be smart about it. Don't want to burn him out. He has to be fresh physically and mentally for the grind of the tour.

It's a business relationship. We're a company: Yzaga-Krulevitz, Inc.

Do we have disagreements? You betcha. Is Jaime stubborn? You betcha. But in the end, he's smart, and ninety percent of the time, he sees my point and adapts.

I'm working all the time. I keep a notebook, and scout out other pro players. I leave it in my hotel room during the day but write in it every night. I talk to other coaches. I get some inside scoops on different players' games. Some of the other coaches like Bob Brett and Gunter Bresnik are cool.

We bring in Jaime's personal physical trainer from Lima, Peru, for ten days. Combine our efforts. Get us all on the same page. We do hot yoga. We do bikram yoga. We are serious about our training but also having fun. There is a time for business and then there is a time for fun.

We're always out practicing something specific. We work a lot on using Continental grip on the serve, overhead, and volleys. We work long hours.

I switch Jaime to VS gut strings and get rid of the Tecnifibre. "Look, you win your first-round match at the Key Biscayne pro tournament, you can buy five hundred sets of VS gut strings," I say to him. "If you win your second-round match, you can afford a massage at every tournament you play."

Jaime ends up winning three matches in Key Biscayne. Sure, one of them is a walkover, but so what. He loses in the round of sixteen to Aaron Krickstein in four tough sets. Krickstein is number seventeen in the world. That's right in the ballpark of where we're aiming to be.

N-I-N-E-T-E-E-N.

Jaime starts to see the light. Invest in your business. And Jaime's business is himself. We get a fitness membership at a health club in Key Biscayne. We do all kinds of classes: cycling, yoga, and ab workouts. We use the fitness machines. Training, training, training.

In May 1989 Jaime beats Pete Sampras in the first round of the West Side Tennis Club in Forest Hills, New York. In the second round, Jaime takes the first set off Yannick Noah, who retires early in the second. Next, he knocks off Sergi Bruguera, followed by Diego Perez. In the semis, he takes out world number 22 — and soon to be French Open Champion — Michael Chang — in straight set. But Lendl mows him down in the final. He is after all number one in the world.

Jaime plays some great tournaments. Three rounds at the Italian Open, three rounds at Roland Garros, quarterfinals in Boston where he loses to Andre Agassi, quarterfinals of Cincinnati where he loses to Boris Becker, three rounds at the U.S. Open where Pete Sampras beats him in four sets, but only after Jaime takes the first, semifinals of Bordeaux where this time he does better against Lendl but still goes down.

In early October, we're back in the States at an ATP event in Florida. Jaime beats Emilio Sanchez of Spain in the quarterfinals before Agassi knocks him off in the semis.

Then the rankings come out — Number 19.

Wow, we did it!

A week later, the computer ranking has Jaime at number 18. Jaime takes off the rest of October from the tour. He has earned it. He needs it. He plays two tournaments in November. In the last one, in Itaparica, Brazil, Jaime makes it to the semifinals where Jay Berger beats him. Berger was ranked number ten in the world.

Jaime's year is done. The year-end rankings come out on December 18, 1989. By that time, Jaime has slipped to number 23, but we had already beaten our goal for the year, by one.

Final singles record, 36-17. Prize money: $182,164 in singles. Final doubles record, 16-11. Prize money: $17,733. Total prize money: one massage shy of $200,000. Not a bad year for a Solomon-sized kid from Lima, Peru. Remember, folks, this is 1989. $200,000 gross is not bad.

After that year, Jaime and I stuck together. This new pro coaching business might just work out after all. Jaime's overall win-loss record on the pro tour was 265-222 and his total career prize money was $2,235,560.

How did Jaime do it? As Mark Twain said, "It's not the size of the dog in the fight, it's the size of the fight in the dog." I wouldn't say Jaime Yzaga was a towering figure by any means. He is only 5'7" and weighs 145 pounds. That is not big by any standard. But how did he beat Pete Sampras who is 6'1" and 175 lbs., Stefan Edberg who is 6'1" and 170 lbs., Boris Becker who is 6'4" and 190 lbs., or Ivan Lendl who is 6'2" and 180 lbs. By the way, all of those are former number one professional tennis players.

How did Jaime beat Andre Agassi in the ATP

Championships in Cincinnati, Ohio? Was it me, the coach? I don't think so. I never hit a ball in any of his matches against Andre, Pete, Stefan, Boris or Ivan. Did Jaime out-fight them? Maybe, but out-compete Andre Agassi. That's a tall order.

So how did he do it? I'll tell you the secret: Jaime Yzaga could eat speed. He could handle power and each of those guys have a lot of power; that is why each spent time as number one in the world. They had weapons. What was Jaime's weapon? Not one of his shots was better or even close to Agassi's backhand, Pete's serve or Stefan's volley. Jaime's shots were not even in the same ballpark. But what he could do, and do well, was eat their speed.

When Ivan cracked a forehand to Jaime, he didn't try to hit it back even harder. If he had, the ball would have ended up in a lake somewhere. When Boris snapped off a 135 mph serve, Jaime didn't try and hit the ball back at 140 mph, or block it with no backswing, no follow through. What Jaime did was he took the pace off the ball. He held his racquet tight like a wall and used their pace against them. And sometimes the ball came back almost as fast. Patience. Patience was his best friend.

Take the pace off and keep the ball in play. That is smart tennis. That is using your brain but more importantly you're playing within yourself. You are not trying to be something you are not. Your ego is left in the locker room.

You cannot out-hit Pete Sampras. Guys tried it every day for years after years, and every time they would lose. But guess what? — These great, great players are only human. When that fuzzy little yellow ball keeps coming back, what do they do? They try to hit harder, to serve harder, to press harder. What happens when they press? They miss. What happens when they miss? They lose confidence. What happens when they lose confidence? I'll tell you what happens: Jaime Yzaga, picks up a win over Andre Agassi, Pete Sampras, Stefan Edberg, Boris Becker, and Ivan Lendl.

***

Casey always said, "A rolling stone gathers no moss." It's great coaching on the pro level. Jaime Yzaga from Peru, Vince Spadea from the United States, Gilad Bloom from Israel, and Tom Shimada from Japan. But then I had a daughter. And I had to decide if I would rather be at her second birthday party or traveling on the pro tour, staying in another hotel that looks exactly like the one I stayed in the previous week. I had to decide whether I'd rather eat dinner alone or with my wife and daughter. Decisions.

With my tennis business back at home, I can still teach. I even help develop some local pro tennis stars, including Reed Cordish and Patrick Osuna. But, ultimately, I need to spend more time with my wife and baby daughter. I need to be there for them. Family is the number one priority.

Chapter 14

The Camp

"My name is Lightning," I say, "and I'm the leader of the camp." I'm looking out at the sleepy campers at the Steve Krulevitz Tennis Summer Camp. It's Monday morning at nine o'clock. U2 is blasting from the Blue Palace (the tennis house) and all the campers are sitting in the shade, courtesy of the E-Z UP tent. The courts are ready.

The tenth and final week of the summer is about to begin. "I'm Lightning!" I shout, to no one in particular. I walk over to my iPod and turn off the music. "This is a Viking camp," I say, as I walk back to my spot in front of the campers.

"Listen up. Quiet!" I say. "I'm the leader of the camp, and next to me are my lieutenants who I will introduce to you a little later on." I proceed to welcome every camper to the camp, individually. I have a nickname for all of them. Then I pull out a piece of paper and ask, "Does anyone know what this is?"

"It's the Viking laws!" Michael "Cannibal" Roth yells out. Back in 1984, when Cannibal was just five years old, his father Alan "Thunder" Roth brought the whole family over for tennis lessons—Nancy "Pinkey" Roth was seven and Amy "Firestar" Roth was three. Today, Michael and Alan of Offit & Roth are two of the most successful accountants in Baltimore.

"That's right, Cannibal," I say. "These laws were handed down by the Vikings, 1,000 years ago and I have them right here."

"What's the number one law of the camp?" I ask next. "Does anyone know?"

"Don't panic!" Chris "Viper" Brill shouts.

"That's right," I say. "Don't panic. That's the most important law at this camp. Whatever happens this week, don't panic. If it rains, don't panic. If it snows, don't panic. If we have an earthquake, don't panic."

"What's camp law number two?" I ask.

"Drink plenty of liquids!" yells Kevin "McHale" Mullaney.

"That is correct," I say. "How long can you last without food?"

"Thirty days?" Carlo "Opi" Olivi says.

Some of these kids have been coming to the camp the entire summer. Others started out as campers but then stayed and became counselors.

"How long can you last without water?" I ask.

"One week," Ricky "The Feiting Machine" Feit says. You remember my first student off the pro tour — Ivan's son, Ricky. Well, he was also one of the first campers at my tennis camp. Now he is a top foot doctor in Los Angeles.

"You won't last until the Olympics on Friday," I say. "But that's not camp law number two. Does anyone know camp law number two?"

No answer. There is total silence.

"Safety," I say. "Campers will not engage in any dangerous or aggressive behavior toward other campers or counselors. Such behavior includes but is not limited to verbal obscenities, slurs, teasing, badgering, physical hitting, pushing, shoving, tripping, chasing, or biting. Any conduct that endangers the safety of another is not permitted. What happens if you break this law? You go to the Box."

I point to a chair off to the side of the fence, near the picnic table. "That is the Box," I say. On the chair sits a cardboard box with the word "BOX" written on it in black magic marker.

"Now, camp law number three," I say. "Drink plenty of liquids."

"What's camp law number four?" I ask. Again, no one says a word. "No campers are allowed in the Blue Palace without permission." The Blue Palace is the tennis house where the Viking Gods — Odin and Thor — stay during the summer. They watch over the camp.

I start picking up the pace now. "Camp law number five: No talking when Lightning is talking, otherwise, you go to the Box. Camp law number six: no drinking from the water jug with your mouth. Camp law number seven: no hitting balls indiscriminately. Camp law number eight: no t-shirts are allowed inside the cooler."

One summer, Ben "Terminator" Bryan unscrewed the top of the water cooler, put his sweaty t-shirt inside, and pulled out a dry t-shirt from his bag. He proceeded to do this until a camper noticed and alerted one of the counselors.

"Camp law number nine: No gambling, drugs, alcohol, or cheating is allowed at the camp. Camp law number ten: No campers can take down the Bat Cave without permission. Also, Lightning, Brian Tobin, Jacques Rogge, and all of the counselors, will protect, defend, and provide a safe environment for the extremely young and helpless campers. Camp law number eleven: Any camper who does not want to participate in 'Watch your back at three o'clock' can find safe refuge inside the Bat Cave. No water can be thrown in there."

"What's 'Watch your back'?" Adam "AJ" Ring asks.

"That's when we throw water on each other at the conclusion of the camp day at three o'clock," I say. AJ nods his head but doesn't seem to totally understand. He will if he stays until 3:00 p.m.

"Camp law number twelve: No climbing trees or fences. Camp law number thirteen: If you order a popsicle for snack then you must eat the pop. If you do not order a pop then you will not get a pop. Camp law number fourteen: This is a big one. If you throw water after time is called in 'Watch your back at three o'clock,' then you will go to the Box. Camp law number fifteen: Thursday is 'Dry Thursday.' That means there is no 'Watch your back at three o'clock' on Thursdays. Camp law number sixteen: Anyone who messes up the bathroom will go directly to the Box. And the final camp law, number seventeen: If you go to the Box you will not get snack." There's a morning snack and an afternoon snack. The morning snack is avatiah—which is Hebrew for watermelon—and chocolate power bar. The afternoon snack is popsicles. If you go to the Box at any time, then you will not get snack the next time around.

"Are there any questions?" I ask. There are, of course,

none because no one has understood a thing.

"Let me give you a brief tour of the Gilman facility. We have nine courts. Over there is the Blue Palace and next to that on top of the picnic table are the Twin Towers," I say, pointing to the two water jugs.

"We have fresh oil from the Gulf of Mexico to drink. We pumped it up from Louisiana. Today we will be playing pick-your-partner doubles. So start thinking about who you want as your partner. The winning team will get a prize Friday morning at 'Breakfast for Prizes.' Tomorrow, we have the Davis Cup, which is when countries compete against countries. I'm leaving early because Brian Tobin is coming in from London to run the Davis Cup. The winning country will also receive a prize on Friday morning." Brian Tobin was the former President of the International Tennis Federation (ITF).

"Wednesday we have Team Competition, which is where you play for your team. You do not play for your school, your family, your church, synagogue or mosque, the city of Baltimore, the state of Maryland, or your country, the USA. You play for your team. You get one point for a singles win and two points for a doubles win. The team with the best name will get an extra point. The team with the most points at the end of the day will win a prize on Friday morning at 'Breakfast for Prizes.' Thursday is Camp Championships, just like Wimbledon and the U.S. Open. If you come in second in your match, you go into the back draw. It's all singles. The winner of the tournament will get a prize. Mano-a-mano. Also on Thursday we have the Pleiadian story with Billy Meier, the one-armed farmer, and Travis Walton. And don't forget Thursdays are 'Dry Thursdays.' That means no water battle on Thursdays. But every other day, watch your back at three o'clock. Friday, of course, is the Olympics. Jacques Rogge will be here from Belgium, and we will have tennis, soccer, football, and 'It's Academic,' all for gold medals." Jacques Rogge was the former President of the International Olympic Committee.

It's Friday. The last day of tennis camp. Last day of Soccer International, too, which is also my camp. Both at Gilman School. That's when things get crazy. All bets are off. No-holds-barred. It's time.

But Marc Hoffman, the Superintendent of Buildings and Grounds at Gilman, is not here yet. How can we do the Trojan Truck Horse Attack against soccer camp if there's no Trojan truck? All week long we've battled the soccer camp. They've attacked us, and we have retaliated. It's Water War. Water guns locked and loaded.

One of their attacks, I have to admit, was pure military genius. They went all the way around Gilman. Still on campus, of course. Snuck up through the woods beside the tennis courts, and their lead general, Robert "Cactus" Wiese, was on us so quick. He jumped on top of the picnic table, where we keep the "Twin Towers," unscrewed the top on one of them, dipped his long rifle (aka water gun) inside, and started firing. He did a lot of damage.

When tennis camp went to attack soccer camp, Flavio Davito came out from hiding in the woods for a rear attack. Very well executed. It was a big win for soccer camp. We were all soaked, but, with the August heat, fifteen minutes later we were dry again.

The Trojan Truck Horse Attack was going to be payback. The tennis commandoes were picked. The final attack was scheduled for 2:00 p.m. Camp normally ends at 3:00 p.m. so this offensive maneuver would come a full hour before then. But it's 2:10 p.m. and there's no sign of Marc or the maintenance flatbed truck.

Thomas "Sprout" Langston is eleven and goes to Gilman. He'll be a commando. He is also an actor and played the Young Boy in the Clint Eastwood movie "J. Edgar." His brother, T.J. is thirteen and will be there for the attack on soccer camp. Ryan "Crocodile Rock" Lombardi is also ready. Born ready. He's twelve. Croc Roc has a Super Soaker that sprays water like a fire hose. Miles "Davis" Calabresi will be a lieutenant in the truck. He goes to Yale. Loves the camp. And is a great leader. We also need a sergeant, so I pick Greg "Sphere" Becker. Aaron "Speedy" Karacuschansky will lead the remaining tennis troops after we pull off the surprise attack. Patrick "Rafter" Gillece will come running in with the bulk of the force. The commandos in the truck will be totally outnumbered, but we're hoping the surprise element will be enough.

I call Marc on his cellphone. "I'm on my way," he says. "Be there in five minutes." Everyone is locked and loaded. Each Water Blaster and Super Soaker is filled. We send a lookout to check on soccer camp and report back. They're still playing on the field, totally clueless. Just like sitting ducks, waiting for the attack. Now it's time for the Viking prayer. We pray to the Viking Gods — Odin and Thor. Then Marc arrives.

The Trojan Truck Horse Attack is a success. The execution is perfect and soccer camp is annihilated. It's a total victory. And just like that another year of summer camp comes to an end.

Chapter 15

Aggravation

Aggravation [ag-ruh-vey-shuh n] n

1: an increase in intensity, seriousness, or severity; act of making 2: the state of being aggravated 3: something that causes an increase in intensity, degree, or severity 4: annoyance; exasperation.

I didn't want to deal with this aggravation. Shortness of breath. Profusely sweating after a cardio workout. Some discomfort in the middle of my chest. I tried to ignore it. By the time my symptoms are worse, it was almost too late.

Coronary Artery Disease. For a professional athlete who has been in shape his entire life I don't even know what that is. Coronary artery disease (also known as CAD) is the most common type of heart disease and the leading cause of death for both men and women in the United States.

A ninety-nine percent blockage of the left anterior descending artery (aka the widow-maker) is more than aggravation. A lot more. The left anterior descending artery supplies over half of the heart muscle with blood. Ninety-five percent do not survive a ninety-nine percent blockage of the widow maker. Believe me, I am not Superman. If I were, I would not have had coronary heart disease. What I am is lucky. Very lucky. I am lucky that I was home that Saturday morning; lucky that I called 911; lucky that the ambulance found my house quickly; lucky that nitroglycerin was available in the ambulance; lucky that Dr. Henry Sun at St. Joseph Medical Center in Towson, Maryland was on call and there waiting for me; and very lucky that I worked out and stayed in shape all of these years because my other arteries bought me valuable time.

On the bright side, ever since my coronary artery disease I'm no longer allowed to shovel snow. Shoveling snow is a known trigger for heart attacks. Cold air constricts the heart arteries and the motion of digging and lifting up a shovel full of snow closes those arteries. That's how you end up face down in the snow, end of story. Every winter, hundreds of people drop dead while shoveling snow. In fact, a person is more likely to keel over while shoveling snow than when running or jogging on the treadmill.

I survived the blockage, took some drug cocktails, and was back in the saddle, back to coaching, back to exercising, and back to thanking the many people in my life who have helped me along my journey.

Chapter 16

The Bottom Line

It's Friday, May 17, 2013 at 8:30 p.m. I'm just getting home after a long day and even longer tennis season. We've just lost the Maryland Interscholastic Athletic Association (MIAA) Championships to Mount Saint Joseph High School. It's my second year as Head Varsity Coach at the Gilman School, a private preparatory school for boys in Baltimore, Maryland.

I walk into the house. Marley, my dog, jumps on me with her wagging tail, wanting to play. Minky is in the kitchen, cooking up some dinner. She doesn't say anything to me about the match. She is smart, very smart, and knows me so well.

"Dinner will be ready in fifteen minutes," she says. Minky works at the Cystic Fibrosis Foundation. Most nights she doesn't get home until after 8:00 p.m. She's by far the hardest worker in nonprofit I've ever seen.

I head upstairs to shower. I've lost before, but losing as a coach is different. It was never a concern of Ann's if I lost a match on the tour. Sure, anyone can lose and come in second. There's no crime in that. Usually after a shower, you feel better. But the lump in the stomach doesn't go away.

Two and a half hours of a very hard-fought MIAA title match. The boys gave it everything they had. The match was held on the courts at the University of Maryland, Baltimore County. The team with the best record usually has the honor — and the advantage — of hosting the title match on their home courts. In our league that was Mount Saint Joseph. But where their courts used to be, a brand-new gym now stands. During the season, they had used the club courts at Atholton, which are pretty good. But it's not the ideal site for a final. So we played at UMBC, a neutral site, instead. It's a very nice facility and a Division I school.

Three singles and two doubles matches. First team with three wins, walks away with the title. The tennis is very high-quality for the East Coast. Especially for Baltimore. We lose number one and three singles. But win number two doubles. It all happens very quickly.

It's 2-1, Mount Saint Joseph. The number two singles match is just beginning the third set, and were up in the third in the number one doubles match. We eventually go down in the third set of the doubles, 7-6. We lose the title.

After the match is over, I get the boys together. "Listen," I say, "we're going to walk out of here in a few minutes, and you have absolutely nothing to be ashamed of. Nothing." I walk over to each player and shake their hands. "Thank you for all your effort and commitment this season," I say. "You boys are always champions in my book. Now let's shake hands with the other team and get out of here."

The days and weeks pass. You try not to go back to that day at UMBC. When you do, you get angry. A tough loss on the tour can stay with you for a few days. But you better get over it fast because next week is a new week and a new tournament. The tour is tough on you like that. But coaching is a different story. Your decisions as a coach affect your players, their parents, and grandparents, and the school.

Gilman School is a powerhouse. It has a fantastic athletic program. Football and lacrosse are big at Gilman. Tennis has a rich tradition. Cal Ripken Jr.'s son, Ryan, graduated after my first season year coaching the tennis team. He was a star on the basketball team and, of course, baseball team. Some of Baltimore's greatest writers, businessmen, musicians, and athletes have graduated from Gilman.

There are 475 students in the upper school. We go up against schools with 1,000 plus kids and beat them. The Gilman boys put it all on the line. They always do.

Over the next few months, I read some coaching books and reach out to a few past coaches. Maybe Keith Puryear from Navy has some ideas, or Chuck Kriese, the former Clemson tennis coach. I use my resources to gain valuable knowledge and develop new strategies.

Then the day finally arrives—May 14, 2014. Twelve months almost to the day from that finals match at UMBC. Gilman vs. Mount Saint Joseph.

Mount Saint Joseph has beaten Gilman in the past two MIAA finals. But this year the finals are being held at Gilman School. The pressure is on. We get one shot. One chance for all the marbles. It's like the seventh game in the World Series.

I'm semi-nervous. So what do I do, panic? Never. I grab a fictional crime novel by Jo Nesbo, a Norwegian crime novelist. The Bat: The First Inspector Harry Hole Novel is a great book.

I'm reading at the table next to the courts when the boys start filtering in for the match. They begin to warm up. I'm still reading. The biggest moment of their high school tennis careers. I look relaxed, and, truthfully, it's because I am. Because this year, no mistakes. Faith, knowledge, and hard work. Win or lose, we have already accomplished much more than last year. The boys see me and, I think, are a little surprised. I'm sitting at the table reading a book before the biggest match of the year. Our season is on the line. Our goal is right there. Three points and we're the champs. I'm not in their faces. I'm not fist-pumping or saying, "This is it. Let's get 'em." Nobody wants this more than I do. I know that might sound silly, but it's true. It's high school tennis, sure. But I have passion. I want it for the boys. I want it for Gilman School—Henry P.A. "Bones" Smyth, the Headmaster; Timothy Holley, the Athletic Director; John E. Schmick, the former Headmaster; Lori Bristow and Nick Petruzzella, the Athletic Trainers, who kept the boys healthy all year.

Garrett "Milkman" Weinstein, our number one player, had a bad shoulder. E. J. "Trout" Abass sprained his ankle twice. Jake "The Snake" Wohl had to serve underhanded in his match because of back and hip problems. Graham "Mister" Duncan pulled his thigh muscle and couldn't even play against Mount Saint Joe in the league match. Cole "Coleslaw" Sutton sprained two fingers on one hand. Coleslaw came to my summer camp at Gilman for the first time when he was four years old, along with his older brother, Cooper "Boo Boy" Sutton, who was six. Now Coleslaw is sixteen years old, a junior at Gilman, and our number two singles player.

I want it for the School, sure. But truthfully I also want redemption. I want to be Genghis Khan today. Destroy all opposition. It's primitive. It's not spiritual. It's a part of me that sometimes I can't stand. The competitive fire. It's exhausting sometimes.

Even though I appear to be reading at the table by the courts, I'm also thinking. I am rehearsing the speech I am about to give to the team. We meet five minutes before the start of every match to go over the lineup, wind conditions, and our opponents. It happens quickly. There is not much time before a match. Only a couple of minutes.

Mount Saint Joseph is on the second row of courts, warming up. Their head coach is in California, so the assistant coach is running the show today. He now has his boys in a circle around him, and he's laying it on, pretty thick and loud. He should be, right? This is their biggest match of the year. He's giving them a long speech. But sometimes saying too much can backfire. Your players are nervous. Or should be nervous, at least at the start. The nerves should dissipate after a few games. If you're not nervous going into a match, then it's a bad sign. That goes for coaches, too.

I walk out to court one. The boys give each other the signal and they all gather around me. Everyone is quiet. I'm sure they're thinking, here comes the "You've got to be a warrior" speech.

"People like the bottom line," I say. "I know I do. So let

me tell you the bottom line here today." I've got their complete attention. The Red Hot Chili Peppers playing on the speaker fades a little into the background. We're all focused. All twenty-four eyes on me. Ten members of the team and the two foreign exchange students, who are the team managers. "Tennis is just a game," I say. "It's just a game to enjoy. So go out there and have fun playing. Enjoy hitting every ball. Don't worry about winning, losing, or the score. Appreciate hitting each shot: forehand, backhand, serve, all of them. Cherish this moment. Suck in the atmosphere. You deserve it. Good luck!" And that's it. No rah-rah speech. Just the bottom line — Tennis is a game. Just play and have fun.

Gilman - 5, Mount Saint Joseph - 0. We are the 2014 MIAA Champions.

Following the team championships each year, the league has an individual championship tournament. Single elimination in each division. The number one singles play against each other, and so on. There are still the five slots: three singles, two doubles. Five total. We sweep all five. It's called "The Whammy." Peace.

May 8, 2015 comes rolling in. The Gilman Varsity tennis team is ready. Only one other Gilman tennis team has won two straight MIAA Championships. This year we are strong with Coleslaw, Trout, Dodger, the River Jordan, Mr. G, Hank,

Foggy. We beat Loyola in the finals. Gilman 5, Loyola 0. The two-peat. Not many high school tennis teams have done it. McDonogh School has. Mount Saint Joseph has. And now Gilman School has.

But here is the kicker — no school in the history of the MIAA has ever won three straight tennis championships. Before the 2016 tennis season, we lost six of our top players. If we are going to have a chance to make history, then we are going to have to pull together and fight like never before. Remember three singles and two doubles. Five points total. We only need three for history.

The final is a rematch against Loyola. They come out hungry for revenge. The match which is scheduled for Thursday gets rained out. On Friday morning it's still raining. By midafternoon, the sky starts to clear up. The Gilman maintenance crew comes out with blowers and driers. We need five courts that are completely dry.

The match finally begins at quarter to five. In all five matches, Gilman wins the first set. But the tide turns. Suddenly, we're in a death struggle. We win one singles and one doubles. But two singles and two doubles go down in a close, but no cigar, third set. That leaves the number three singles to decide the Championship.

It's now 8:10 p.m. and pretty dark out. The last singles

match is tied. We decide to stop and resume on Sunday. The next two days seem like two months.

Sunday finally rolls around. Our singles player wins. We beat Loyola, 3-2, and become the first team ever to capture three straight MIAA titles.

Then in 2017, we become the first team ever to win the MIAA Championships four years in a row. It's the four peat and Gilman School once again makes history.

***

During the 2016 tennis season, I was honored at the United States Professional Tennis Association (USPTA) Annual Convention as the 2015 Mid-Atlantic High School Coach of the Year. USPTA tennis professionals, which can be either head tennis professionals or assistants, must be at least eighteen years old, pass the on-court and written exams, and complete stages one and two of youth tennis coaching. In addition, USPTA pros should be able to organize and implement tennis programs, recruit and develop players, direct and assist with pro shop management and facility maintenance, and conduct private and group lessons.

The Convention is a three-day event. A smorgasbord of tennis knowledge all gathered in one place. One very nice place — The Woodmont Country Club in Rockville, Maryland.

The seminars at the Convention are worthwhile. Speakers fly in from all over the country. They give presentations on a variety of areas—budgeting your tennis facility, positive coaching, fitness routines for advanced players, cardio tennis, and injury prevention, just to name a few.

At the Awards Luncheon, I am presented with the 2015 USPTA Mid-Atlantic High School Coach of the Year award. I accept the award on behalf of the boys at Gilman School. It's true and special honor. Before accepting this award, I never really saw myself as a high school tennis coach, especially one who approached his job with passion and all-out effort. But you know what, now I cannot imagine devoting this stage of my tennis life to anything else.

###

AFTERWORD

Lightning In A Bottle

A party for Steve Krulevitz at Gilman School? You mean Steve Krulevitz from Park School? At our archrival Gilman? What's next, the Joker inviting Batman over for milk and cookies? I figured it might be a trap. So, there I stood inside Gilman School's Lumen Center, scoping the room for evil henchmen who might be lurking. It seemed all clear, but I wasn't sure I knew exactly what a lurk looked like.

Slowly the crowd and the good vibe filled the room. And the 25 Year Reunion of the Steve Krulevitz Tennis Program held on July 11, 2009 began. Ann graciously offered me the chance to speak. I declined. I'd leave the remarks to the camp guys, stand my post, and watch Steve's back. Turned out there was no need. The only thing that happened was a great time.

But, there's this. I can't let the evening and sentiments pass without comment. The stories told were wonderful. A remarkable twenty five years. But, Steve and I go back five decades. There's more to it. So, here's some context, perspective, and perhaps a capstone.

My first sighting. At the time, I don't know who Steve is. Both our families belong to the Chestnut Ridge Country Club. My dad and I walk onto the court to hit around. I see a kid playing a few courts over. He's clearly about my age, which is nine. On the other side of the net is a guy I know to be the best player in the club. This grown man, who is a terrific player, is struggling to keep the rally going. I'd never seen anybody like me, play anything like that. I just stare at him and wonder, "Who is that guy?" My dad and I start at it. I'm swinging away, but pretty much, I'm preoccupied with rubbernecking the action on the court down the way. I see the man walk off. He's replaced by a girl. She's older than we are. And taller. The back-story is quickly apparent. It's the kid's older sister. The parents obviously have prevailed on him to play with her. He's not happy about it. The kid says, "Forehand." He hits her one. She nets it. The kid says, "Backhand." He feeds another to her. She sprays it. The kid says, "Overhead." He sends up a lob. Frame job. "You stink," the kid says and he walks off. I'd never seen anybody like me say anything like that. So I go, "Who is that guy?"

The next year, I returned to Park School and our relationship began, as classmates, teammates and lifelong friends. Tennis was a constant in our lives. Steve, of course, went on to play on the pro tour. I became a lawyer and agent for the players. Along the way we'd shared all the best times. (Steve, Ann and I all went on their first date. Though he and I have varying takes on how it transpired.) Steph's birth. Steve being inducted into the Maryland Sports Hall of Fame. Our wives becoming wonderful friends and colleagues. My stepson Jerome morphing into "Murray" and playing at Steve's summer tennis camp. You get it, a long list. And the tough ones too. Illness, injury and the loss of family and treasured friends.

On to our nicknames. He may be Lightning to all of you. But to me he's Dave. And I'm Doc. The handles come from our respective favorite TV shows, circa 1967. His was "The Invaders." Roy Thinnes plays David Vincent, who alone knows that creatures from outer space have landed and launched a plot to take over the earth. In each episode, tries to convince a disbelieving world of their scheme. My pick was "The Fugitive." Like the subsequent movie, it's about a surgeon, Dr. Richard Kimble, falsely convicted of murdering his wife, and the quest for justice and freedom. Hence, Dave and Doc. Of course, Dave remains a renowned extra-terrestrialologist (yeah, I know that's not a word), while my prospective medical career tanked somewhere around calculus.

Now, you may think you know what a terrific athlete Steve, Lightning, Dave is. But you don't. He's even better. I know. I was there.

Dick Wallace, was the Park School Athletic Director for, well, what seemed like forever. Despite all those years and the countless athletic games, only one photograph occupied the center of his office wall. That picture captured a moment, not a Varsity sports game, but a sixth grade soccer match. We were playing a Catholic Youth Organization. In that photo Steve was midway through dribbling past the entire opposing team, and scoring an unassisted goal. I'd never seen anyone do that. Detecting a pattern here?

Basketball. Steve was the point guard on our undefeated championship team. I like to think I helped him get there. All those one-on-one games in his driveway on Claran Road. Kicked my butt. Let's just say, I helped build his confidence. Of course, it wasn't always pretty. There was the great Park-McDonogh rumble. It all started when Steve subjected his guy not only to tenacious ball-hawking defense, but also inflicted the dreaded "mouth guard treatment," wherein Steve, up-close-and-personal, repeatedly flicked the offending devise between his lips. The taunting worked. Maybe too well. The guy lost it, threw a haymaker, and off we went.

Spring sports. Steve won the MSA tennis title four times. The team, not so serendipitously, was founded the year he became eligible. Maybe you knew that. But, how about this? By our junior year, Steve was so much better than everyone else, he no longer practiced. Instead, he also played on the lacrosse team. Led the State in scoring actually. Then he was off to All-American honors and a pro career.

To be a great athlete (or great at anything) requires monocular devotion. It necessitates a world view with a center on self. Unfortunately, it leaves many forever stunted. They never outgrow their egocentrism. Therefore, it is all the more remarkable, that the cocky nine year old boy I first encountered on the courts of Chestnut Ridge, grew up to be a man of such great empathy and generosity of spirit. All the more praiseworthy that, despite traveling the globe and playing at the pinnacle of the sport, his greatest achievements came not on the grass of Wimbledon, or the clay of Roland Garros, but on the sun baked asphalt of Baltimore, where he touched, inspired and changed so many lives for the better. Steve, Lightning, Dave take your pick. I am proud to call you him friend.

– Rick "Doc" Schaeffer

Printed in Great Britain
by Amazon

61377573R00119